NEW YORK, U.S.A.

This book is dedicated to the youth of North Belfast,
with all the best hope for their future.

Lighting technician: Bryan Tarnowski   Prop stylist: Rachel Hornaday

For information about permission to reproduce selections from this book,
write to Permissions, Houghton Mifflin Harcourt Publishing Company,
215 Park Avenue South, New York, New York 10003.

www.hmhco.com

Library of Congress Cataloging-in-Publication Data
McGarry, Jack
The Dead Rabbit drinks manual: secret recipes and barroom tales from two
Belfast boys who conquered the cocktail world / Jack McGarry, Sean Muldoon,
Ben Schaffer; photography by Brent Herrig.
pages cm
ISBN 978-0-544-37320-4 (hardcover); 978-0-544-37339-6 (ebook)
1. Cocktails. 2. Dead Rabbit Grocery and Grog (New York, N.Y.)
I. Muldoon, Sean. II. Schaffer, Ben. III. Title.
TX951.M154 2015   641.87'4—dc23   2014043215

Book design by Steve Attardo/NINETYNORTH Design

Printed in China

C&C 10 9 8 7 6 5 4 3 2 1

The Dead Rabbit Grocery and Grog

DRINKS MANUAL

SECRET RECIPES AND BARROOM TALES FROM TWO BELFAST BOYS WHO CONQUERED THE COCKTAIL WORLD

SEAN MULDOON • JACK McGARRY

and BEN SCHAFFER

Photography by BRENT HERRIG

HOUGHTON MIFFLIN HARCOURT
BOSTON • NEW YORK • 2015

CONTENTS

INTROD

UCTION

Sean Muldoon and Jack McGarry launched and ran one of the best bars in the world. And then they did it again.

What follows is a celebration of two bars. We will learn about the Cocktail Bar at the Merchant Hotel—elegant, first-class, an international destination, historically-focused, with an exacting standard of service—and the Dead Rabbit Grocery and Grog—a neighborhood haunt, ragtime piano venue, pretensionless spot for a pie and a pint, which nonetheless manages to embody all the aforementioned virtues of the Merchant, too. The creative forces behind them were the same two men.

Sean Muldoon is a bar mentor, one of the first of his generation to see the opportunities in the cocktail revival. He takes his place as a taste bud traveler in time, an adventurer of absinthe and sailor on the high seas of sours and slings, an excavator of elixir erudition, a man who made his mark on moonshine.

Jack McGarry is the consummate barman in the flesh. It is he who tamed the tincture tiger and deciphered the lost language of the Ancient Cocktailians. Discovered after years of slumber in a block of hand-shaped ice in the basement of Jerry Thomas's Exchange Saloon, he is said by some to be the only nineteenth-century barman alive today.

In both their establishments, the boys from Belfast have focused on historical drinks. At the Merchant, the emphasis was on the twentieth century heyday of British and European hotel bars, where travelers would encounter classics, perfectly made with meticulous detail. Once that was accomplished, they ratcheted up the challenge. At the Dead Rabbit, the drinks still come from history, but they are not the classics, they are the forgotten ones: Drinks that have long since fallen out of fashion but can still teach us much about flavor and texture, not just as it was understood in bygone eras, but in ways relevant to our own tongues and nostrils.

However, even as we begin to create myths, let's dispel one. While Jack and Sean are both meticulous barmen and bar historians, and their respect for their antecedents is at the core of everything they do, the drinks in their bars and in this book are not just instructions out of old books. They haven't simply been selected and reprinted here. Everything in this book is an original recipe, though it was inspired by historical sources. As you will see, every drink listed in this volume includes the historical source material from which it was derived. But these recipes are all-new renditions, not only updated for modern ingredients and the modern palate, but enhanced, deepened, awoken through the inspiration of our authors.

The reverse is also true: unlike the many encyclopedic cocktail manuals on the market, we are only including original recipes that you won't find elsewhere. We will tell our own stories here. So pull up a stool, unclip the nutmeg grater from your belt, and let's start our tale.

HOW TO OPEN THE BEST
BAR IN THE WORLD, TWICE

Tales of the Cocktail, 2010

The sky darkened, the planets paused in their headlong course, and man-kind held its breath as Sean James Muldoon entered the ballroom of New Orleans' Roosevelt Hotel. This Irish barman, representing his Belfast estab-lishment, the Merchant Hotel, had been nominated for the most prestigious award in his industry—World's Best Cocktail Bar—at Tales of the Cock-tail's 2010 Spirited Awards, the Oscars of the beverage world. Meanwhile, back in Belfast, his right-hand man and head bartender, Jack McGarry, was handling Saturday night service. Well, someone had to mind the shop.

In each of the three previous years that Tales' highest award had been given, a New York City bar had been its recipient. New York was then cap-ital of the cocktail world, and everyone knew it. In 2009, a new category had been introduced to the Spirited Awards—Best American Cocktail Bar—so the New Yorkers could win something and still give the rest of the world a chance for World's Best. Instead, New York bars swept both categories.

Several other categories had been added in 2009 to the fast-growing Spirited Awards, including World's Best Hotel Bar. That award, plus those for World's Best Drinks Selection and World's Best Cocktail Menu, went to a little-known outfit from a small town not usually found on hospitality's international stage: Belfast's Merchant Hotel. Who were these characters?

Belfast, 2006

When pub magnate Bill Wolsey opened the Merchant Hotel in 2006, it was only the second five-star establishment in Belfast's history. The elab-orate mocha-colored Italianate pile on Waring Street in the redeveloping Cathedral Quarter, formerly the Victorian-era headquarters of Ulster Bank, was a symbol of the new Belfast, eager to benefit from the Good Friday Agreement and get on with the day-to-day of a city: its arts, commerce, and street life.

Belfast had never seen anything quite like The Bar at the Merchant Hotel. Wolsey wanted his hotel's main bar to be just as grand as the Corinthian columns lining the building's entrance. Remarking on his experience there a couple of years later, cocktail historian and author David Wondrich characterized the hotel as "elegant, but not swank." It had all the touches that displayed culture and none that displayed crass consumption. Pictures hung everywhere, of every size and style, just as one might accumulate over time in one's own house.

Red velvet chairs, shining wallpaper, dark wood, glowing chandeliers, and gilded portraits of recumbent ladies were just the beginning; Wolsey wanted the service and the selections to be top-flight as well. Accordingly, he contacted Sean Muldoon.

ARDOYNE—MARSEILLE—ABERDEEN—LONDON—BELFAST

Sean had already built a reputation as Northern Ireland's preeminent bartender and cocktail creator. He had grown up around pubs and bars, but hadn't initially seen this as a career. Raised during the stunning daily violence of the Troubles, what he most wanted to do with Belfast in his youth was escape it.

The Catholic working-class neighborhood where Sean grew up, Ardoyne, in north Belfast, was surrounded by Protestant areas, making it a flashpoint for killings by all sides of the conflict. When Sean was a boy, bomb threats and street closures by the British Army were so common that sometimes he would invent one as an excuse for coming home late.

This atmosphere of aggression made a big impression on young Sean, and after he left school at sixteen he felt his ambitions would be best served by the army. But as Northern Ireland was part of Britain, that would have meant the British Army, and no Catholic boy from Belfast could join up with the forces of the oppressor. Of course, there was the Irish Army of the Republic to the south, but they similarly took a suspicious view of Northerners in their ranks.

Belfast was not a city of opportunity; growing up, Sean knew many people chronically out of work, and as a young man he struggled to find work himself. Usually work meant a few months on a building site in London if his uncle could hire him, otherwise it meant the dole. Sean earned a reputation among his friends since, as the only non-drinker among them, he made his unemployment allowance of thirty pounds a week last the longest.

So, at the age of twenty, Sean did what many young men without opportunity had done for centuries, and shipped out to Marseille to join the French Foreign Legion. After several training exercises in the rain, he acquired a chest infection, consequently failed the fitness exam, and shipped right back. He realized that fighting and potentially dying for a foreign country was not among his goals. But there seemed to be so little for him at home.

While sitting on a beach in Marbella in southern Spain, on his way home by the scenic route, Sean couldn't help but notice its tranquil beauty compared with the confusion and clashes of Belfast streets. He felt trapped by the idea of returning to Belfast, and thought about how much easier it would be just to walk into the warm, inviting Mediterranean until everything faded away.

But if the sea was so inviting, if Spain was so different, maybe he could simply free himself from the trap. Escape Belfast, and live a life elsewhere. He wouldn't have to rely on any army to get him out; he would save his pennies, as he'd always been good at, with that day in mind. And he would use his money to create something meaningful. He had always loved music, foundational rock like Lou Reed, Neil Young, the Stones, the Who, the Kinks, Jimi Hendrix. Music had been something that made sense, in a world that rarely did. If he raised some money, he could make a record of his own, tell his own dreams. When he returned to Belfast, his friends thought he was nuts. Putting to one side the small facts that he didn't know how to write music, sing, play an instrument, or know any musicians, he remained determined.

But if the sea was so inviting, if Spain was so different, maybe he could simply free himself from the trap. Escape Belfast, and live a life elsewhere.

In the newspaper, Sean found a hotel bar job that offered live-in accommodation. The hotel was in Banchory, Scotland, eighteen miles west of Aberdeen on the way to Balmoral, the Queen's residence in Scotland. It might not be Mediterranean beachfront, but it was a start. Living in the hotel would make those saved pennies pile faster. And getting away from Belfast, even if not as far as he had originally envisioned, would almost be like acceptance to a writers' colony.

But he was turned down for that job, and several like it, because he had no experience. Undaunted, he signed up for work experience in the bar trade, which meant working for free in a bar, but receiving another ten pounds a week onto unemployment. It also meant you didn't have to go to the dole office every two weeks to "sign on," always an embarrassment for young Sean.

After a few stints in different pubs, Sean landed at the Chicago Pizza Pie Factory, a dream of Americana developed for the British public by an American expat. The creamy, dessert-like cocktails were ahead of their time for Belfast in the early '90s. And, better than that, the bartenders shared their tips.

A year of job training later, he was accepted to Scotland, to the same Banchory hotel he had applied to before. His first discovery was that in Banchory, and perhaps even the rest of the world, there was a concept called "hospitality," which meant that service industry employees were nice to guests. This was unknown in Belfast at the time; you were served your beer by bartenders and servers exhibiting the same professional aplomb of any bus conductor or discount store cashier. In Banchory, he witnessed people nodding and smiling as they passed pints to punters, and he realized that this could be part of the secret recipe for success in his industry.

Sean had written all the lyrics for his album of original music during his time in Scotland, and found a collaborator in composer and performer Bill Campbell.

After his time in Scotland, Sean returned to Belfast, working in a social club his father used to frequent, the Crumlin Star, while "doing the double" by still claiming unemployment. He had saved up £8000 from the Scotland sojourn, all intended for the musical project, not for daily living. He only worked there for a few months, but in that bar he met Anne, who would be his wife.

Sean had written all the lyrics for his album of original music during his time in Scotland, and found a collaborator in composer and performer Bill Campbell. On the resultant CD, *Warhead: The Bereaved*, Sean told of the sectarian struggles of Belfast, but he and Campbell, a Protestant, showed their yearning for peace. (Of course, for the Muldoon completist, this rare album is an essential acquisition.)

The alternative pleaded for by *Warhead* did not come to pass at once, not for Sean. He began working as an assistant manager in a pub owned by a friend, located in the Catholic Cliftonville Road area. It might not be the place to roll out world-class customer service, but it was a job. Although the bar was frequented by Catholics, it was nonetheless right near a Protestant neighborhood, making it an easy target for sectarian gunmen. The clientele even jokingly acknowledged this, referring to it as the "Ceasefire," as it had opened during that period of the Troubles. The more macabre among them called it the "Sitting Duck." The Ceasefire's proper name was the Clifton Tavern, and its position made Sean uneasy. He told one regular not to sit in his favorite seat by the door, because he'd be first in the line of fire. As the winter holidays came closer, Sean was even more wary. It would be an easy time for violent sectarians to find victims.

. . . the Irish National Liberation Army managed to kill Wright with a smuggled pistol during visiting hours.

A reciprocal ceasefire between the Irish republicans and Ulster loyalists had been declared in the fall of 1994, but it did not last. IRA bombings resumed in London and Manchester when the British Government failed to negotiate. In Belfast, angry loyalists roamed the streets, looking to create terror of their own. However, the IRA reinstated the ceasefire in July 1997, when negotiations that would lead to the Good Friday Agreement began. But many splinter groups did not want peace.

Loyalist leader Billy Wright, who was suspected of taking part in more than twenty murders but convicted of none, was finally put in prison for threatening a woman's life. While he was being held, on December 27, 1997, prisoners from a breakaway republican group known as the Irish National Liberation Army managed to kill Wright with a smuggled pistol during visiting hours. Wright's group, the Loyalist Volunteer Force, swore revenge, announcing that every Catholic man, woman, and child walking the streets was a potential target.

Bars in Belfast had security: metal grilles, locked doors, and an intercom with a camera for bartenders to choose whom to let in. None of these accommodations were at the "Sitting Duck." As New Year's Eve approached, Sean felt more foreboding. He knew the killers liked to choose important days on the calendar, for the bonus of a holiday that would be forever ruined for those left behind.

Sean was the day manager, and as he handed over to the evening man on December 31, Sean told him not to take his eyes off the door. The man laughed. A couple of hours later, as Sean ate a late meal with his fiancée in a

nearby French restaurant, men entered the Clifton Tavern and opened fire. They killed Eddie Treanor, who had been sitting by the door and had never been in the bar before that night, and seriously wounded five others, one of whom would also eventually die from his injuries.

After that, Sean felt lost all over again. The world was out of control, and he could not control it; he was neither a diplomat nor an army man. He was just a bartender.

At work, Sean kept imagining the scene of New Year's Eve over and over. He thought he was hearing noises in the dark. Sean asked the owner to keep a second member of staff on at night so Sean would not have to lock up alone, but the owner didn't want to spend the money, and threatened Sean's job if he didn't stop fooling about. Sean quit.

During his second bout of unemployment in the industry, Sean happened to watch a television documentary about a cabinetmaker from Italy. He was a simple man from a small town, but his family believed he had a special skill in making the most beautiful furniture. His uncle took him to America, where he became a sought-after designer of furniture for the rich and famous. Sean was fascinated, thinking of his own father, a woodworker who gave no special effort and received no special acclaim. Sean decided that if he was to have a trade, and if it was to be bartending instead of music, then that was what was within his control. If he was to be a bartender, he would aim to be the best he could—the best there is.

MULDOONI THE GREAT

Sean began training for the heavyweight title of best bartender in the world. He took pub management and wine classes, where all of the other participants were sommeliers and managers studying at their employers' behest and largesse. One of his fellow students said if Sean was serious about being the best, he should work for Jaz Mooney.

At that time, Mooney owned a few bars, but he was opening many more, and he was doing so differently. Sean visited one of Mooney's bars, Madison's, and was more than impressed. Instead of metal grilles and intercoms, there were men in overcoats who held the doors open to you, welcoming you. The barmen and waiters were in uniforms, with white jackets. The drink menu included six white wines and six red wines by the bottle. They had an espresso machine, whereas the Belfast norm was Nescafé out of a jar. And they had cocktails. Sixteen of them, each in its own unique glassware.

At that point, the only cocktails Sean had heard of were Sex on the Beach, which in a world bereft of cranberries was served as vodka, peach schnapps, and orange juice; and a Black Russian, a measure each of vodka and Tia Maria, topped with Coke. And here at Madison's, they didn't just have more cocktails than he knew were possible, they had the exotic liqueurs needed to make them: Midori, Galliano, Rumple Minze.

Sean immediately sent in his résumé to each of the pubs Mooney owned. The general manager of Madison's, Peter Campbell, was from the Cliftonville Road area, and knew of Sean's experience with the Clifton Tavern. He sympathized with Sean, and gave him his opening despite his lack of experience and poor upbringing. Sean began his new life as a cocktail bartender, with his first wage packet of £108.

Morgan Watson! The Canadian wizard of modern mixology, like a James Bond of the bar, with women swarming him and his every move reported in the press.

As Sean reveled in the new menu and environs, one name was increasingly heard around the bar as rumors swirled: Morgan Watson was returning. Morgan Watson! The Canadian wizard of modern mixology, like a James Bond of the bar, with women swarming him and his every move reported in the press. Watson had traveled the world in search of inspiration, and he was returning to Belfast to assist in opening Mooney's latest venture, the Fly.

When Sean met Watson, he appeared from the mists in a purple T-shirt and black combat trousers, looking like the globetrotting, leading man of action he was. He introduced himself in his deep North American voice, and Sean knew this guy was different. And what made him different from ordinary men? Cocktails! Sean knew that to be the best barman in the world, he first had to be better than Morgan Watson.

To promote his work, Sean entered whatever drinks competitions were available, testing his new interest in cocktail making, not just cocktail shaking. In the '90s, that was mostly through the Bartenders Association of Ireland, an old-fashioned group still honoring the glory days of Fern Bars. Sean entered in 1998 with a drink called Havana Ball (get it?) featuring Havana Club Gold rum, mint, apple juice, lemon juice, and balls of stem ginger. Simple by today's standards, but advanced for its time. Mojitos were popular, and this was a new dimension for a mint drink. But the winning drink, formulated from Havana Club, Baileys, peach schnapps, grenadine, and cream, was gloriously entitled Pink Fluff. The judges were picked randomly from the audience, and the nineteen-year-old girl who tried the Havana Ball made a face.

Within Mooney's company, Battle of the Bars competitions were staged between each venue. Because of the talent at those bars, it was the biggest competition in the country. This meant Sean went up against Morgan Watson more than once. Unlike the staid Bartenders Association contests, these were extravagant pageants, involving scenic design as well as costumes. Sean, naturally, competed in top hat, cape, and magic wand as Muldooni the Great. Morgan Watson was typecast as a Canadian Mountie, and they met at last in the finals. As Sean waved his magic wand over his drink—a blend of Smirnoff Citrus vodka, limoncello, crème de pêche, watermelon, and Champagne sorbet, arranged in a flute with an orchid hanging off the side—all the girls in the audience ran forward, screaming, "We love you, Muldooni!" They tossed their knickers at Sean, exactly as he had planned when he purchased the economy package of knickers that afternoon.

Asked by a friend how he thought he did, Sean answered with confidence that he had won. A judge within earshot felt this was poor form, and Muldooni came second to the Mountie.

LEARNING LONDON

Sean asked Watson what he needed to learn. Watson's answer was clear: "London." Sean became a fast study of the cocktail revival then sweeping the capital, traveling across the Irish Sea three or four times a year just to spend a fortune in bars in the name of research. He became particularly fascinated by London's tradition of exquisite hotel bars, a factor that seems almost part of the definition of the city. When profiled in the UK's bar business magazine, *Theme*, Sean was asked what person, living or dead, he'd most like to work with. He cited Salvatore Calabrese (alive), then of the Lanesborough Hotel on London's Hyde Park Corner.

Salvatore Calabrese, with his courtly charm, traditional black suit, and precise mustache, was the epitome of the Continental bar host. His stomping ground, the Library Bar at the Lanesborough, was a majestic upholstered grotto of leather armchairs, heavy curtains, and Calabrese's collection of ancient cognacs in discreetly locked cabinets.

Besides the old style glamour and grace of the location, the Lanesborough had special meaning for Sean. On one of their trips to London, when he was walking by Hyde Park with Anne, she suffered a panic attack. He brought her across the street to the hotel, knowing that an ambulance would get to it faster than to two nameless wanderers on the street. And indeed it did, with the paramedic treating Anne at the scene, before they headed in for a deserved cocktail (Sean and Anne, not the paramedic).

When the Lanesborough public relations office read Sean's statement in *Theme*, they invited him to spend two nights as their guest in the exquisite hotel, working side by side with the Maestro himself. It was the pivotal opportunity Sean needed to witness and absorb an expert working his craft in his native environment, the environment he controlled with flips of a shaker or a wink at a longtime customer.

> *This was not just smiling at the customer, which had been revolutionary to Sean back in Banchory.*

Besides the stunning bar craft on display, the working-class boy from Ardoyne was dazzled by Calabrese's world. As soon as he walked into the lobby, he ran into national acting treasure David Jason stalking through the lobby just like his famous sitcom character Del Boy. While Sean checked in at the reception desk, Sacha Baron Cohen, in costume as his character Ali G, was framed in a doorway. This is a wonderland, Sean thought.

The wonders escalated within the confines of the Library Bar. Standing nervously in his new white jacket, Sean met the Maestro. Immediately, Calabrese said, "You're the guy who liked my cocktail." He had remembered the one time they had met, six months earlier in a crowd of a hundred, where Calabrese had given a cocktail presentation based on fresh juices, and challenged anyone who didn't like tomato juice to try his special nonalcoholic version of a Bloody Mary. Sean had, in fact, liked it, and Calabrese remembered. This was not just smiling at the customer, which had been revolutionary to Sean back in Banchory. This was a total commitment to the craft. Then football manager Terry Venables came in for a few drinks, and Calabrese and new assistant Sean were off to serve him.

As he polished a crystal glass, Sean decided that he must join this world.

Back at Madison's, Sean was now creating innovative new menus based on the ideas he picked up in bustling London. The first was called "Around the World in Eighteen Stays," with drinks inspired by countries around the world, such as Australian Barrier Reef and Thai Massage Parlor. Each drink had a mini description, "Uncover the depths . . . of the Australian Barrier Reef," sort of like tropical drinks menus in the Tiki era.

Sean also made his mark on bar décor and promotion. When Smirnoff Ice held a contest for the best bar display of their product, Sean pounced. He bought a mannequin, but just the top half, and positioned it as if it were coming out of the mirror in Madison's back bar, complete with jagged cracks in the surface as it emerged. One half of the mannequin was in half a suit and tie, and the other half was crazily painted with glitter, an aggressive animal. That half clutched a bottle of Smirnoff Ice, the potion which had caused the transformation. Around the bar were Smirnoff Ice bottles dressed as Winter Olympians, and Spice Girls dolls repainted to be Ice Girls. It was a marketing bullshit tour de force. They won the contest, and Smirnoff's parent company Diageo used the images on their global website, promoting it as one of the best back bar displays in the world, the yardstick against all else would be judged. Art students came to photograph the work on a daily basis.

Keeping his finger on the pulse of the London vanguard was still crucial, and Sean continued to visit the metropolis with Anne. He took her to a bar called the Player in Soho especially because he knew it was owned by the same people as the brand-new (and much harder to infiltrate) Milk and Honey. While schmoozing the bartender to get a reservation at Milk and Honey, Sean perused the menu before him. The Player had a concept called In-Flight Upgrades, where the spirit in your drink could be traded for a more premium brand in return for a more premium price. They called the levels Economy, Business Class, and Club Class. Sean dug it.

But not quite as much as he dug Milk and Honey. They arrived in the downstairs bar and, again, it was a new experience. He witnessed bartenders creating drinks using egg yolks and nutmeg—drinks which actually tasted good. What was going on? They cut ice by hand. Glasses and even cocktail shakers came from freezers. The drinks were beautiful, but dry, not the fruitiness he was familiar with. It merited further study, so he talked himself into a job there for a few days, purely for the reconnaissance opportunity, much as he had in his initial days of £10 per week "work experience."

However, as Jaz Mooney's empire grew, it was becoming more centralized, with purchasers deciding what products would be available in all of the bars, and therefore what drinks could be created. Sean was hitting a ceiling. In his intense desire to be the best, he had gained a reputation as "Serious Muldoon." In human resources interviews, when asked what he did in his spare time, his answer was reading books on management and trying out new cocktail recipes. And when describing awards he'd won, he'd be sure to mention the ones he didn't win because he was robbed, or where the judges didn't know anything. So Serious Muldoon left, creating his own cocktail consultancy, The Perfect Drinks Company, the first of its kind in Ireland.

Sean helped set up Mooney's newest competitors, exotically named bars such as Zen and Opium. For his work at Opium in 2002, Sean was inspired by a London bar called Lab, all fresh fruit, all purées. Sean took the award-losing Havana Ball, put it in a beautiful bamboo glass, and called it the Siamese Sling. It quickly became the most popular drink in the bar. Customers even asked for it in other bars in Belfast. Belfast tastes were catching up with Sean's own.

The bars Sean helped create won a string of national awards, and as his notoriety spread, Sean was asked not just to design bars and menus, but to speak to industry groups. He agreed, but never felt quite comfortable doing it, having no experience with public speaking. Eventually he felt serious stage fright, to the point where he was no longer confident even in picking up the phone, in case it was another speech engagement. Just as The Perfect Drinks Company was picking up steam, Sean choked. He decided he needed a break from the limelight, a chance to recharge. Once again Belfast seemed too small. He took the bartending equivalent of a commission in the Foreign Legion and signed on with Radisson Seven Seas Cruises.

The drinks were beautiful, but dry, not the fruitiness he was familiar with. It merited further study . . .

For nearly five months, the six-star liner cruised through the Caribbean, South America, and up through Baja California. Sean tended bar on the observation deck during the day, with intermittent and somewhat indifferent customers. A bright spot was one guest he met every day, an elderly, jovial character from Colorado named Harry Harrison. Harry Harrison was single, and he went on a cruise every year. He was an inherently optimistic guy, and even serving him his Ketel One vodka martinis made Sean feel better about life. Finishing his tour on the cruise liner, he considered a second trip through Asia, but instead realized it was time to marry Anne and make a life at home again.

Sean was back on terra firma. He was ready for Bill Wolsey.

BUILDING THE BAR

"Let me run the bar as I see fit, and I promise you it will be the most talked-about bar in the world." Such was Sean's vow to Wolsey and his

management team, and he meant to keep it. He didn't quite know how at that point, but he knew it was going to happen.

The Merchant was still an empty building site, but when Sean first entered it, he immediately saw the potential. Instead of leaving the country to find a place in the cocktail world, here was all the glamour of London brought to his doorstep. Sean imagined creating a bar with the exuberant grandeur of the Lanesborough's Library Bar and the elevated craft experience of Milk and Honey. He wanted to create a cocktail bar in a hotel, rather than a hotel cocktail bar.

Imagining the spectacular bar that was to come, Sean began planning the perfect menu to serve there. Drawing on classic cocktail manuals from the 1930s and '40s, he was particularly inspired by Charles H. Baker's *Gentleman's Companion* (1939), *Trader Vic's Bartender's Guide* (1947), and the quintessential Lucius Beebe's *Stork Club Bar Book* (1946). Realizing that a great hotel must be great at whatever hour its guests require, the first Merchant Hotel Bar Book took a cue from Beebe and sorted by time of day: Morning at the Bar, Afternoon at the Bar, and Evening at the Bar. (How much more evocative those daily periods seem when the final three words are added.)

Each section had its salutatory quotation, such as this choice morsel from Joseph Hergesheimer's *San Cristobal de la Habana* (1920), where the author encounters a daiquiri: "Unquestionably the cocktail on my table was a dangerous agent, for it held, in its shallow glass bowl slightly encrusted with undissolved sugar, the power of a contemptuous indifference to fate; it set the mind free of responsibility; obliterating both memory and tomorrow, it gave the heart an adventitious feeling of superiority and momentarily vanquished all the celebrated, the eternal, fears." Wake up, sleepyheads!

From there it was Corpse Revivers and Picker-Uppers, Milk Punches and Eggnogs, Fizzes, Sours, Toddies, and Champagne Tonics. After the presumptive nap it was Afternoon at the Bar, with Cocktails, Swizzles, Cobblers, Sangarees, Daisies, Fixes, Cups, Shrubs, and Punch bowls. Following a second planned or unplanned loss of consciousness, one would be refreshed and ready for the Evening: Aperitifs; Flutes; Coolers; Highballs; Sparkling Sours, Slings, and Mules; Juleps, Smashes, and Muddled Drinks; and Tropical Drinks. It was a mixed drink overview of rare breadth, offering libations worth investigating for the neophyte and old hand alike. Many of these drink categories had not recently seen barroom light. Yet it was the Tropical Drink, a particularly out of fashion style, where Sean wanted to make a splash.

The Merchant had on hand some supremely old spirits, and when they came into play, the Platinum price could be inflated indeed . . .

He had determined to carve out a fourth section in the Bar Book, based on the In-Flight Upgrades from the Player, for what he termed the Connoisseurs' Club. This was another listing of classic cocktails, but each was available at three price points. The Silver level was a delicious, well-made drink. The Gold level upgraded the rarity of its base spirit. And the Platinum brought its level of luxury and expense to absurd, or one might say five-star, heights.

In the example of a rye Manhattan, Silver saw it made with Van Winkle 13 Year Old for £8.45. Gold was the Sazerac 18 Year Old for £13.50. And Platinum brought on Rittenhouse 21 Year Old for £75. The Merchant had on hand some supremely old spirits, and when they came into play, the Platinum price could be inflated indeed, as in the Old Trimbook bourbon from 1937 used in a £175 Mint Julep or the Pendennis 1905 bourbon in a £195 Old Fashioned.

These were expensive cocktails by any calculation, but they would not hold the record for World's Most Expensive Cocktail as determined by the *Guinness Book of World Records*. To achieve that, Sean would have to look further.

Sean sought a particular prize, a bottle of J Wray & Nephew 17 Year Old Rum, the same rum used by Trader Vic in his original Mai Tai, which had not been bottled since the 1950s. Sean began asking around the industry for clues about this elusive bottling. Unbeknownst to him, others were also on its trail. The UK brand manager for J Wray & Nephew at the time, James Robinson, had asked Master Distiller Joy Spence about the 17 Year Old during her visit to the Notting Hill Rum Festival earlier that year. Due to the recent increase in the popu-

Sean began asking around the industry for clues about this elusive bottling.

larity of Tiki bars and of the Mai Tai cocktail in particular, would J Wray & Nephew ever consider reviving the 17 Year Old? Spence said that wasn't in the cards, but that they had recently found twelve bottles of the rum during a worldwide inventory. She offered to send him some. Robinson received six of the twelve bottles a few months later, with an attached letter indicating that four bottles were to be given to notable UK figures for their contributions to the rum industry: Ian "The Rum Ambassador" Burrell, cocktail expert Ben Reed, brand ambassador *par excellence* Angus

Winchester, and Appleton rum cocktail competition winner Glen Hooper. The other two bottles were left to Robinson to hand out as he pleased.

Those two bottles sat on his shelf the day Sean called. Shortly, one was bound for Belfast.

So the rarity of rarities went behind the bar, and ultimately into a glass with curaçao, orgeat, rock candy syrup, lime juice, and ice as the Connoisseurs' Club Platinum Mai Tai at the attention-grabbing price of £750 a throw (about $1400 at the time). In its own elaborate ceremony, the Guinness organization officially named it the world's most expensive cocktail in 2008. Of course, "most expensive" is sometimes more easily achievable than "best," and that first award has changed hands several times since, with the current holder as of this writing being a drink almost ten times as costly. But the chance to drink a bit of history—not just a new drink with expensive ingredients, but an original cocktail as it was otherwise no longer possible to experience it—was unique to the Merchant's Mai Tai.

The accolades began to pile up for Sean's vision. Both *Theme* and *Class* magazines, the preeminent British chroniclers of the industry, presented the Bar at the Merchant Hotel with their top awards in 2007 and 2008, including *Class*'s "Best UK Cocktail Experience." However, across the Atlantic, at Tales of the Cocktail 2008, the bar was up for three awards. It lost them all.

ICE

"Many years later, as he faced the firing squad, Colonel Aureliano Buendía was to remember that distant afternoon when his father took him to discover ice." So reads the famous first sentence of *One Hundred Years of Solitude,* by Gabriel García Márquez, in its masterful English translation by Gregory Rabassa. When the chapter ends with the young Colonel and his father encountering ice for the first time, the elder proclaims, "This is the greatest invention of our time."

Ice can be an obsession of the craft cocktail bartender. They like it in hard-to-achieve shapes, such as perfect spheres or enormous cubes. They like it shaved into snow. They like it hand-chipped to order. But mostly, they like it large and crystal clear.

From the beginning, the Merchant drink program was heavy with housemade ingredients. Fresh juice squeezed daily was a given. In their pantry they made apricot liqueur, cherry liqueur, ginger beer in old stone bottles, and even experimented with bottle aging spirits. But ice had to be right above all.

There are many approaches to achieving beautifully clear, impurity-free

ice. Unfortunately, they don't work. To determine it scientifically for themselves, the Merchant team dedicated a room and started a laborious regime of trial and error—the fruits of which you can now reap within these pages.

Sean filled the Merchant Hotel's basement with chest freezers and began to experiment. He and his team tried metal pans, but they warped during freezing. They settled on plastic Gastronorm pans, about six inches deep. They quickly discovered that too many trays in one freezer took too long. And there needed to be room for cooling air to circulate over the trays, so you couldn't just stack them on top of each other, you had to stagger the stacks. In the middle of this experiment, a fire inspection mandated that the freezers had to be removed from the basement. Without missing a beat, Sean had them installed in an abandoned building across the street, also owned by Wolsey.

They tried expensive bottled water but there was no advantage. In fact, telling the customers that the ice was made from Fiji Water resulted in their asking to see the Fijian icebergs that were being flown in.

Sean and his team even discovered that using distilled water, a favorite of many bartenders due to the lower level of impurities, didn't make a huge difference in the resulting ice, because the ice was open to the impurities in the air as it froze. However, the way ice froze in the plastic pans was from the outside in and bottom up. During freezing, the impurities tended to stay in the not-yet-frozen bit, getting pushed to the center and top of the block. The Merchant's solution: to wait until everything was frozen but the very center, and to cut that part out with all its impurities. This delivered the cleanest, clearest ice from normal tap water. But it did require a watchful eye over the couple of days needed to freeze the large trays.

They determined that when the ice was nine-tenths frozen, still with a bit of water sloshing around on top, the optimum time had arrived for cutting it for bar use. Cut with a bow saw into large strips, the ice was then stored in the freezers until it was ready to be shaped for different uses. Chipped ice was delivered for Mint Juleps and tropical drinks via ice pick. Cubes were carved from the strips with a carving knife, and their purity was a source of special pride to the Merchant team. It was, simply, beautiful.

To customers, it was a source of delight, but sometimes confusion. One customer sent back her gin and tonic because it didn't have ice in it. Sean took the drink back to her and pulled out the cubes with tongs, showing that in fact there were three large cubes, mostly invisible due to their clarity. And more than once a confused customer, wondering where the ice was, ended up pulling the heavy cubes out and dropping them back in, breaking the glass.

When Hidetsugu Ueno, a world-famous bartender known for his meticulous process, was introduced to the Merchant ice program, its setup as well as its result, he declared it was the finest he had seen. To this day, few have recreated what Sean was able to do in the abandoned building across the street from a five-star hotel.

SHAKING THE SOPHOMORE SLUMP

With the launch behind them, Sean was already thinking about a second edition menu. And he was determined to avoid the "second year blues," where your subsequent efforts never match up to your initial success.

The *Merchant Hotel Bar Book Volume 2* was unafraid to dive deep into history. Not just a bar user's manual anymore, it became a scholastic overview of drink history. Organized by drink category, much as the first Dead Rabbit menu would be several years later, it contained many of the same actual types of drinks as the previous volume, but in a manner that described the grand diversity of the booze pantheon. While the first menu had been oriented towards the needs of a hotel guest, the second menu focused on the tastes of a cocktail connoisseur in a world-class cocktail bar.

Sean continued to find inspiration in 1940s books like the *Stork Club Bar Book*, but also the 1941 cocktail guide *Here's How*, a tourist item produced by the Asheville, North Carolina, pottery shop Three Mountaineers for a bit of variety in their catalog. (The book was reprinted several times, including as *Just Cocktails*.) The Asheville volume was between carved, hinged wooden covers to fit with the rustic Appalachian goods of the Three Mountaineers, and Sean borrowed that style of cover for Bar Book Volume 2, except with a more elegant finish in keeping with its translation to a five-star hotel.

Bar Book Volume 2 begins with Punches and makes their connection to fruity Cups, before venturing into Sours and Daisies, Fizzes, Hot Drinks, Highballs, Juleps and other muddled drinks, Cocktails themselves, and nonalcoholic concoctions. At the back is the familiar Connoisseurs Club (now without the possessive) where a few J Wray & Nephew potions are still available at the record-beating price. Throughout the book an emphasis is placed on adding the sparkle of Champagne to many drinks, in keeping with the bar's place in such rarefied surroundings.

Also drawn to the magnetism of the Merchant was a young bartender named Jack McGarry.

Beginning to move away from familiar contemporary categories and towards historical drink categories, Sean, in Bar Book Volume 2, paved the road that the Dead Rabbit would march bravely down a few years later. With its breadth, depth, and above all, delicious recipes, the Merchant Hotel Bar Book Volume 2 was crowned "World's Best Cocktail Menu" at Tales of the Cocktail 2009, where the bar also won "World's Best Drinks Selection" and "World's Best Hotel Bar." Far from a slump, Sean had delivered exultation. In 2008, the Merchant had failed to be honored with Tales' awards, and one year later, it swept them.

THE CONNOISSEURS CLUB

Sean had always promoted the Bar at the Merchant Hotel as a cocktail bar with rooms, rather than as the bar of a grand hotel. But with the vindication of his strategies at Tales, he was ready to take the Merchant to a global audience. In those days there was less transatlantic cross-pollination of bartending ideas, and the Merchant was a pioneer in starting that conversation. Tales of the Cocktail had largely been an American-only gathering up to this point, but due to the Connoisseurs Club, bar folks came from London and even the European continent to see what was happening.

First a destination for locals, then for travelers from the UK and Ireland, the Merchant's reputation grew. Until its appearance at Tales, it had been largely unknown elsewhere on the planet. Sean instituted a seminar program in 2007 in coordination with Steven Pattison of liquor industry design agency Drinksology—to be known as the Connoisseurs Club, after the Merchant's cocktail list for the discerning palate—and invited bar luminaries from around the world to participate. Every few months a different

speaker—industry sages like Audrey Saunders, David Wondrich, Dale DeGroff, Gary Regan, Simon Difford, Jeff Berry, Ian Burrell, Wayne Curtis, Robert Hess, Tony Conigliaro, and Sasha Petraske—would come to discuss, demonstrate, and serve different historical drinks of their special area of study.

Each sage spoke on his or her particular area of mixed drink expertise, while the Merchant's stalwart crew formulated and passed out the very drinks under discussion. In 2008, David Wondrich made his presentation on "a boozy look at the life of and drinks of 'Professor' Jerry Thomas," in conjunction with Gary "Gaz" Regan, the cocktail adventurer and raconteur who spoke on the topic of drinks that have no business being made, and yet somehow still pique our fancy.

Breen told Sean that he saw incredible potential in Jack, but Tatu was closing, and Jack was planning on going back to university.

And when each expert returned home, they spread news of the Merchant.

Regan and Wondrich passed hours at the Merchant's bar, but also slipped down the street to a proper old-fashioned pub called the Duke of York.

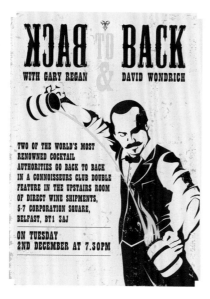

With its decor of tin Guinness signs and a bar made from brick paving, with poetry inscribed on each step of its stairway, it seemed the perfect quasifantastic Irish pub. The kind of place where you have never been before, but you can still come to and be welcomed.

Also drawn to the magnetism of the Merchant was a young bartender named Jack McGarry. Born in the same north Belfast neighborhood as Sean, he too had originally taken to the trade merely as a way to earn his living. Jack's first job had been at an Irish pub/sports bar known as the Hunting Lodge, but he quickly moved onto Café Vaudeville, the sort of "cut above" establishment that's known in Belfast as a "style bar." Jack's first real experience with high-end cocktails, though, was his next gig at Tatu, where he worked for accomplished bartender Kieran Breen, who had previously worked under Sean at the Merchant. Breen moved with fluid grace behind the bar, but he still knocked out the drinks fast. Just as Sean had realized upon his earlier exposure to these techniques and recipes, Jack knew this was what he wanted to do.

After Jack made repeated attempts to contact and impress Sean, who felt he wasn't ready, Breen finally interceded on his behalf. Breen told Sean that he saw incredible potential in Jack, but Tatu was closing, and Jack was planning on going back to university. If Sean didn't give him a chance at the Merchant, one of the greatest future bartenders might be lost forever. Thus was Jack finally brought into the fold as a trainee at the Merchant.

Sean was meeting some friends at the Spaniard, a local pub, when Jack approached him. Jack thanked him for the opportunity and Sean returned to his friends. "Do you not know who that is?" one of them asked him. "That's young Jack, Jack McGarry's son. Do you remember playing cribby on our street all those years ago?" Cribby, an urban ballgame involving throwing a ball at the curb and catching it as it bounced back, with higher scores for executing many complicated bounce-and-catch combinations, had been Sean's passion as a lad. He played on a neighboring street where he was the champion. He and his mates would play all day, only "stalling the ball" if an old lady was crossing the street or a car came by, blocking the field of play.

Every Sunday, cribby would be interrupted as Jack McGarry, Senior, would ride by on his bike to visit his own father, with Jack McGarry, Junior, strapped into the infant seat. Sean would restlessly watch them sail by, before resuming his championship of the cribby league. So he had in fact met future partner Jack McGarry when he was one year old.

Back in the twenty-first century, tropical drink maven, mogul, and *macher* Jeff "Beachbum" Berry arrived for his Connoisseurs seminar talk in 2009. David Wondrich recommended him for the opportunity, and recommended to Jeff that he take it. Berry arrived a day early and immediately bellied up to the bar, where he was shocked at the variety on offer, including their well-curated selection of tropical drinks. But mostly he remembered that while he had previously encountered *sprezzatura* style bartenders who make the difficult look easy, he had never witnessed a bartender with such laser-like focus on his work as Jack McGarry. After spending the night after his Connoisseurs presentation in the Merchant's bar, Berry had arranged to stay an extra night to see some of Belfast. But he stayed in the bar that night as well.

Jack excelled in this seductive environment, learning the tricks and suggesting his own. It wasn't long before he was Sean's full collaborator, working with him to create the third edition of the Merchant's celebrated mixed drink menu, which for the first time categorized drinks more by how they were used than by how they were made, such as drinks of the "elegant and refined style," "rich and fruity style," "long and refreshing style," and "short and potent style."

Sean trusted Jack to manage the bar as he considered their next move. He thought about how the visitors loved the Merchant's elevated program, but they also loved the straightforward, welcoming feel of the neighboring Duke of York pub, too.

TALES OF THE COCKTAIL, 2010

In New Orleans at Tales 2010, the Bar at the Merchant Hotel, in the tiny town of Belfast, beat a crowded field to take home the prize of prizes, the numero uno, World's Best Cocktail Bar. Sean phoned Jack. "We fucking won the fucker."

Sean had worried he'd have to leave Belfast to fulfill his ambitions. But it was Belfast that had nurtured his success.

Where could he go from here?

Back in Belfast, Jack too was wondering what came next. Winning the awards at Tales seemed like the cap on their careers at the Merchant. As the hotel expanded, so too did its staff and its corporate structure. Jack wanted to work in a bar where his efforts were focused exclusively on being as creative as he could for the benefit of the customer. Not necessarily having meetings with the corporation's director of quality. Was there somewhere else that might serve as a platform for Jack and Sean's kind of work?

Belfast was still giving. Providentially, Sean had recently met Conor Allen, a native of Connemara, County Galway, who was part of a financial software company that had just been sold to the New York Stock Exchange. Traveling back and forth between Manhattan and Belfast, Allen began to see the Bar at the Merchant Hotel as the best place to relax, catch up with friends, and feel at home. Conor became particularly enamored of a minty Ketel One Mai Tai variation that Sean had called the Mister Harrison in honor of his cruise ship guest. As Conor would regularly bring business associates, sometimes a room full of them, to sample the wares, Sean knew they had arrived when an order for thirty Mister Harrisons came in.

As Conor learned more about cocktails and hospitality from the Merchant, he also realized that for all its high-tone bars, New York lacked anything approaching the Merchant's magic courtesy of Muldoon and McGarry.

Conor Allen, with a combination of Irish pride and a canny eye for investment, suggested that Sean think about New York as the next bar

venue. This came at the right time for Sean; he felt he'd taken the Merchant just about as far as he could. They'd won every award imaginable, they'd helped reinvigorate the city, and they'd raised the profiles of Jack James McGarry and Sean James Muldoon. They had already built the best bar in the world. New York had a certain appeal as fertile ground if one were to try again.

And wasn't it New York where the cocktail had originally flourished in its late nineteenth-century zenith? Wasn't it New York where the first celebrity bartenders were consecrated, men like Jerry Thomas and Harry Johnson? And, indeed, wasn't it New York whose history of that era had had a strong participation from the Irish? If he needed a bar concept, the Irish in New York offered a compelling story to tell.

OLD SMOKE

In 1850s New York, lower Broadway was the home of opulent hotels, restaurants, and members' clubs outfitted for the city's gentry: the Astor House, the City Hotel, Delmonico's, and the Century Club, for just a few examples. But just east (near today's Foley Square) was the now-disappeared neighborhood of Five Points, where the other half lived. This area, through to the East River waterfront, was where the unruliest saloons in town held sway: The Hole in the Wall, John Allen's Dancehall, The Slaughterhouse Point, and, of course, Kit Burns' Sportsman's Hall, where the main attraction was gambling on how many rats a dog could kill after it was thrown into a pit full of them.

Lower Manhattan was a dangerous brew of larcenous violence, blood sport gambling, and waterfront debauchery—all ruled by that infamous Irish street gang, the Dead Rabbits, and their leader John "Old Smoke" Morrissey.

Morrissey, a bare-knuckle boxer who ultimately became a United States congressman, with a certain amount of murder and terror in between, seemed to Sean to embody the American dream for many of his countrymen.

Born in Tipperary, Ireland, in 1831, Morrissey came as a child with his parents to Troy, New York, later arriving in Manhattan when he was 18. Beginning as a prize fighter, he soon took over the Dead Rabbits gang, leading them into many street confrontations with his nemesis, William "Bill the Butcher" Poole, and his own gang, the Bowery Boys. The Bowery Boys, born in the United States, resented the newcomers (despite being no more than a generation or two removed from Europe themselves). As historian and novelist Peter Quinn would write in his introduction to the first Dead Rabbit mixed drink menu:

> Poole and Morrissey indulged in fisticuffs at least twice, and although the accounts are unclear, it seems Poole came out on top both times. On February 24, 1855, they bumped into each other in Stanwix Hall, a newly opened saloon on Broadway, near Prince. Morrissey spit in Poole's face and pulled a pistol, but it misfired. Bill the Butcher unsheathed his knife. Luckily for Morrissey, the police arrived and broke up the fight. The affair was finally

settled when associates of Morrissey returned that evening and shot Poole in the heart. He lingered for two weeks before uttering his parting words: 'Goodbye, boys. I die a true American.'

Morrissey himself gained the nickname "Old Smoke" earlier in life when an opponent in a bar brawl knocked him into a stove, searing his back against the hot coals. Despite his wounds, Morrissey got onto his feet and thrashed his foe.

When the Dead Rabbit gang wasn't simply killing people, they executed creative schemes like helping newly disembarked countrymen with their bags, which they never saw again, before suggesting a hotel at which they would be kidnapped and held for ransom. (Creativity aside, this was not a method of hospitality which inspired Jack and Sean's bar.)

Gambling, theft, and the occasional bout brought Morrissey fortune, though more gambling then lost it for him. He simply made the money over again. Throwing his lot in with Tammany Hall, he served them in the New York State Senate, and later was elected to two terms in the United States House of Representatives. As Quinn notes, "at his nomination, the editors of the *New-York Tribune* wrote, 'the public decency and the dignity of the national legislature have seldom been so boldly outraged.'"

However, at Morrissey's funeral in Troy in 1878, there were 20,000 mourners, including the entire State Senate. Morrissey was 47.

The more he read about Irish history in New York, the more Sean realized that the Irish American experience there, where high and low were both drawn to Lower Manhattan in search of spirits of appropriate character, was a terrific bar concept. He was reminded of American guests at the Merchant, who toasted its cocktail bar but nonetheless also enjoyed the simpler charms of the Duke of York pub down the road. Why not a bar that did both parts well? Plus, both the exemplar pub and New York City itself were named after the same guy, the Duke of York. It could not have been clearer. The two-in-one concept would be brought to New York, and it would be the Dead Rabbit.

Every Man Jack

Jack always thought ahead, whether it was about recipe trends or his own career. He had already begun to consider how to build on his experiences at the Merchant, but when Sean approached him with the Dead Rabbit idea, Jack hadn't been expecting such a monumental change.

Another city, another continent even, new partners—and, most importantly, a bold, new concept.

Jack had assumed he'd be involved in another upscale cocktail bar, but when he heard the Dead Rabbit concept, which was both parlor and pub, he knew immediately it was right. It would take the highfalutin cocktails and make them hospitable again.

Even though bartenders had already begun their still-ongoing obsession with original "startender" Jerry Thomas, the resulting bars still tended to be of a non-Thomas speakeasy type, hidden away and often for members only. While bars might focus on drinks from the Prohibition era, or the mid-century rise of Tiki, or even Thomas' own late nineteenth-century heyday, Jack wanted to go further back. He wanted to incorporate every important milestone starting from the dawn of convivial drinking. And he didn't want the fruits of his labors to be only for the gentry, or the manager's friends.

When Jack had first started at the Merchant, Sean had told him to study the cocktail manuals by the best living bartender-theorists, Dale DeGroff and Gary Regan. He further recommended the twentieth-century bar books that had inspired him, such as those from Lucius Beebe, Trader Vic, Charles Baker, Harry Craddock, and Ted Saucier. Jack had absorbed all their works and then plunged into the listed bibliographies to follow the thread back to earlier guides. With the Dead Rabbit on the horizon, he knew he'd have to learn a lot more about pre-twentieth-century drinking. He raided those bibliographies again, as well as the exhaustive recipe trove of the excellent CocktailDB.com web resource.

Sean and Jack decided the time had come to leave the safe haven of the Merchant. Even though they had no new bar to go to yet, they knew they needed to put all their efforts into making that new bar come about. Sean would move to New York to lay the foundation. Jack didn't see much point in staying on at a job he (and all his coworkers) knew he'd be leaving soon enough. But there was no bar for him to tend in New York yet. So they found him a berth at Milk and Honey in London, where he could work and hone his skills further for the short while before the Dead Rabbit's opening. Sean estimated about six months would be needed, placing the opening in April 2011, in the Chinese Year of the Rabbit.

Rabbit Hunting

Everyone loved the idea of a cocktail bar based in New York called the Dead Rabbit. But, for a long time, the idea was all there was to it.

As a resident of the Financial District, Conor Allen was familiar with Stone Street, a couple of blocks crammed with bars and restaurants, a respite in the middle of the office towers. And he'd become friends with Danny McDonald, the Portlaoise-raised Irish pub impresario who co-owned several of those establishments, plus other well-known pubs around town like the Swift Hibernian Lounge and Puck Fair. Conor asked Danny to act as an advisor, to help them navigate the unfamiliar market.

In Sean's research into early American taverns, he determined they required five elements: a public barroom, a quieter room reserved for VIPs, a meeting room for clubs and societies, a kitchen for food, and rooms for travelers to stay the night. This time they were staying out of the hotel business, but the Dead Rabbit still needed the first four.

The Parlor was Sean's name for the rarefied quarters for cocktail consumption, just as would have been found on lower Broadway, where the elites met in sumptuous surroundings. It would be their version of New York's glittering hotel bars of yore, or indeed the Merchant's own cocktail bar.

The public barroom came to be known as the Taproom. This would be an informal setting, in the style of the waterfront dock bars that would have been the respite of working men and women. It would have a raw bar, pub grub, craft beer on draft, and a selection of whiskeys of the world. This was the Hole in the Wall, the grog shop, the Duke of York.

Ideally, the bar would also have an Occasional Room, a devoted space for private events, so that the main bars would never have to be shut down for parties.

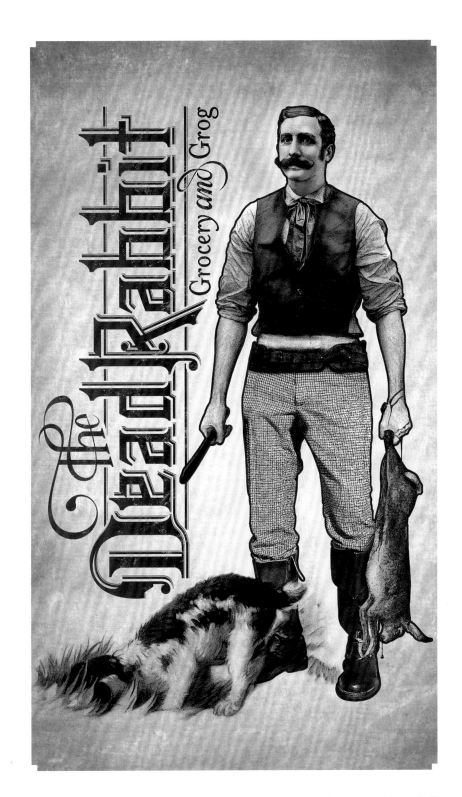

The Dead Rabbit
Grocery and Grog

The problem was finding twenty-first century Manhattan real estate that could accommodate this vision.

Speed Trials

In London, Jack's collection of antique cocktail manuals approached and then quickly exceeded five hundred volumes. He found himself thinking back again and again to what David Wondrich had written in his introduction to the second chapter of *Imbibe*—"For nearly two hundred years, from the 1670s to the 1850s, the Kingdom of Mixed Drinks was ruled by the Bowl of Punch"—and he knew that communal punch, the epitome of convivial drinking from bygone eras, should form the cornerstone of their new undertaking.

In the meantime, he was very much stuck in the present, working almost every day at Milk and Honey as its most junior bartender. Recognized as possessing one of the most rigorous cocktail programs in the world by critics, fans, and Jack himself, Milk and Honey was a boozy boot camp.

At the Merchant, Jack was in control of everything that happened behind the bar. He had whatever resources he needed to create the recipes he wanted. During his employment at Milk and Honey, he was the new recruit on kitchen patrol, and constantly reminded of his status by everyone else. It reminded him of being singled out by a teacher in grammar school, who told the whole class that he had failed his chemistry exam. At that point, he decided he would never give anyone that opportunity again, and never failed another test. He knew he could take whatever his colleagues at Milk and Honey dished out.

A purported photographic memory makes some of his stunts possible, like having your drink waiting for you before you've made it all the way to a seated position.

A lot of what they dished out was even more tests. In the midst of shaking a cocktail, Jack might be confronted with a manager sidling up and popping a quiz: "What year was Coca-Cola invented?" (1892, boss.)

Jack began to think of the Merchant as a Rolls-Royce: elegant to look at, but not the most efficient under the hood. Jack's goal at the Merchant had been to produce the finest drinks in the world. He and Sean had been inspired by the world-class, historical programs at famous London hotel bars like the Connaught, the Lanesborough, the Dorchester, the Savoy, and Artesian. Every detail of the production of the drinks was exhaustively researched and created, from the syrups and tinctures that went into the drinks, to the ice, to the presentation.

But in this pursuit of perfection, speed was not one of the goals. Jack's insistence on working on each individual drink until it was perfect sometimes infuriated other bartenders, as well as Sean and Bill Wolsey, the owner. But Jack didn't care how long someone had to wait for a drink, only that it be perfect when it arrived.

At Milk and Honey, Jack needed to run an efficient bar in order to survive. In fact, the Milk and Honey's Red Room, which seated thirty customers, was streamlined about as far as it could get: one person performed all the duties within. That person had to open the door for guests, seat them, take their order, make sure their tables were clean and candles were lit, send and pick up kitchen orders, refill water, tally bills and make change, and of course concoct the actual drinks. And for his months of work there, that person was Jack McGarry.

He learned to shave seconds off his performance. For example, lighting a candle took ten seconds. But relighting a candle that had recently gone out tended to take only three seconds. So he'd keep some lit candles on deck. Waiting times were crucial, and there was no one else to blame.

While he learned his technique and showmanship at the Merchant, the Red Room did much to make Jack the speed and efficiency expert he is today. Instead of only one dimension of perfection, Jack came to realize that for a truly world-class bar focused on hospitality, you needed both quality and speed.

Having survived this one-man band approach to service, he learned another thing: the way the Red Room was run was not the way to run a bar.

FAIRYTALE OF NEW YORK

All along the way, Jack received regular updates from Sean in New York by email and phone. After a while, it became clear to Jack that the most recent updates, although still regular and detailed, weren't reflecting much actual progress. The estimated six months passed, and then another six, and the bar was no closer to its launch date. There was no location selected. Was there even enough money to make it happen?

Still Jack continued his research into period drinks. He filled notebook after notebook with illegible scrawl that led his girlfriend to call them the "kill the president diaries," after the kind of records that always seem to be left behind by the accused man after some violent tragedy. But in this case the hieroglyphics were the augurs of good fortune.

After a particularly oppressive shift at Milk and Honey, Jack decided he had relit his last candle. He called a local friend, Henry Besant, to see if he had any work going. Besant and partner Nick Strangeway were among the most highly regarded cocktail consultants in the United Kingdom, and their new project was the bar in the renovated St. Pancras Renaissance Hotel, formerly the offices for the railway at St. Pancras Station, but originally opened in 1873 as a hotel. Returning matters to their nineteenth-century state being Jack's current interest, he signed on.

On the very same block at the Dead Rabbit, the historic Fraunces Tavern, where George Washington had held the fare-well dinner to his troops . . .

Working with Besant and Strangeway was another brick added to Jack's foundational knowledge. Agreeing with Wondrich's assessment of the primacy of punch, they put it front and center in their menu, and Jack was impressed with their methods of reconciling centuries-old recipes with modern tastes and practices. But the project was only one of many for the partners, and there were certain limitations working for a large, corporate client that reminded Jack of why he had left the Merchant. He wanted to take what he had learned and implement it in his own bar, his own sandbox for his own constructions.

He needed the Dead Rabbit. He didn't need any more no-progress updates. He just needed it to happen.

THE TRAP CLOSES

Sean and his New York partners looked at dozens of empty bar spaces all over town, focusing on the Flatiron District where bars had begun to appear due to the saturation of the East Village, generally considered the most desirable bar neighborhood. Further downtown, Chinatown and the Financial District were also considered. The Financial District, which incorporates Wall Street and the World Trade Center but no cocktail bars, was thought by some to be too far from the action to appeal to discerning cocktail customers.

For a while, the leading contender was a space on Irving Place, on the

edge of the nightlife-focused East Village, featuring two rooms with separate street entrances. Sean thought that could be set up with the proper Taproom/Parlor divide. The immediate neighborhood, with existing bits of history like Pete's Tavern, seemed suitable. But the property was quite large, and besides the loss of intimacy, something didn't feel right.

No longer content to wait on the sidelines, Jack arrived in New York with ten dollars and his recipe notebooks. Win or lose, he was there to see it through.

Conor had brought fellow investor Kyle Tuskey to the project, but it soon became clear that opening a bar in Manhattan, which neither had done before, was going to be more expensive than they had anticipated. Danny introduced them to his business partners, Peter Poulakakos and Paul Lamas, with whom he owned several restaurant and bar projects in the Financial District, including Harry's Café and Steak and Ulysses'. To keep Sean and Jack afloat as the project wound on, Peter and Paul agreed to find them jobs working in other bars they owned. Jack felt that perhaps it was also a chance for them to be auditioned in a real world situation, since their reputation was known in New York but no one had actually seen them in action.

In New York, Sean and Jack's downtime was spent the way other people might spend it, but for entirely different reasons. They went to bars. But they went to learn. No detail was too small to be noted and considered for use at the Dead Rabbit. And due to their interest in old-time establishments, they spent a certain amount of time at P. J. Clarke's on Third Avenue and 55th Street.

The storied 1884 bar was known for its no-nonsense approach to classic beverages, above par hamburger, and frequenting by generations of celebrities from Jackie Kennedy to Johnny Depp. For the decade or so that he stood behind it, the bar was also known for Doug Quinn, who grew to become the favorite bartender of *New York Times* romantics. (The headline to Frank Bruni's 2010 profile refers to him as nothing less than "the Bartender of Your Dreams.")

Quinn is a bartender in that strictest sense: he tends to the bar, to the needs of its residents. Effortlessly working the huge after-work Midtown crowds, keeping everything snappy, he nonetheless remembers his regulars and anticipates their needs. A purported photographic memory makes some of his stunts possible, like having your drink waiting for you before you've made it all the way to a seated position. But much of his charm is reliant on, simply, his charm. Whether the customer is a Wall

Street suit or someone's mother, a wink and a few warm words are what they need.

Here Jack realized the trinity of bartending: the attention to detail and quality in the drink itself, as exemplified by their program at the Merchant; the relentless speed needed to deliver that quality; and that special bartender's art, the charm of the friendly soul making the delivery. So Jack raised his head from staring down at the mixing glass in his hand to meet the gazes of his customers.

The pieces were in place. But there was no place yet.

WATER STREET

Sean escorted Peter and Paul on a cocktail bar tour of the East Village, showing them the venues he had come to admire on previous visits to New York, and explaining what he wanted to contribute. One stop was Angel's Share on Stuyvesant Street. Opened in 1994, it was the very first of the bars of the current New York City cocktail revival. Focusing on well-crafted classics and plenty of rules designed to keep the space intimate (no standing, no groups larger than four, no loud talking), it also happens to be behind an unmarked door on the second floor of a Japanese *izakaya*.

While taking in its ambience, Peter mentioned that he owned a building with a similar setup. There was a burger shop on the ground floor and a bar up the stairs. He was in the process of evicting the burger tenant for nonpayment of rent, and planned to turn it into a pizza parlor. Maybe the second floor would be of interest to Sean as a side project while they kept looking for the Dead Rabbit.

Sean mentioned the building to Danny, who went to look at the funky space on Water Street in the Financial District. A five-story 1828 building with historically-protected exterior, it had originally been built as a counting house, but the ill-fated burger joint was still in evidence. With its tiny floors, creaky stairs, and poor condition (plus the expense of renovation within a protected façade), it seemed too frail for the muscular Rabbit concept. To Danny, it also seemed perfect.

The block of Water Street where the building resided would have been prime Dead Rabbit gang territory. In their day, before advancing landfill, Water Street had been the docks. Gang members would have roamed outside its door in search of victims. It was the perfect place to tell the story of the Dead Rabbit, right on history's doorstep.

Taproom on the ground floor. A natural transition, via stairs, to the

Parlor. Occasional Room on the third floor. And two more stories for the various laboratories needed to craft ingredients and store inventory. This was 30 Water Street, near Broad Street, in the Financial District.

Construction began and dragged on. Having never built a bar before, and certainly not in New York, Jack and Sean were only now introduced to magically sliding timescales and how a day's work might take weeks to complete. But slowly the bar came together, and Danny felt confident enough to suggest a tentative window for the grand opening: November 2012.

However, as the Federal Emergency Management Agency blithely states on its website, "On the evening of October 29, 2012, Hurricane Sandy made landfall in southern New Jersey, with impacts felt across more than a dozen states."

In Lower Manhattan, the deluge was felt far, wide, and deep. Avenue C in the East Village, where Sean and Jack were staying, had become a tributary, although more than a block inland from the river. At first, when they saw taxis hydroplaning down the avenue, it seemed a comical adventure. The whole area, including their apartment, was without power, water, or heat, and would remain so for days. But they were on a higher floor and were used to enduring some adversity. Then they decided to make the trek down to the bar to see how their lives might really be affected by the storm.

On the tip of Manhattan, where the bar was located, the storm was at its most calamitous. The nearby Paris Café, first opened in 1873, had been almost totally destroyed (it would spend 51 weeks under renovation before its triumphant return). On the very same block as the Dead Rabbit, the historic Fraunces Tavern, where George Washington had held the farewell dinner to his troops, suffered not just a flooded basement, but a further two feet of water pushing into the ground floor. Equipment, as well as food and beverage inventory, was lost in restaurant basements all over the neighborhood.

And the high-rise office towers that defined the neighborhood stood empty. Without power, their workers were relocated, often with no specified return date, while the buildings were repaired. For the local restaurants, even if they could reopen, where were the customers?

Among the ruin, the Dead Rabbit seemed to be saved. Its basement had flooded, but as it had not yet been finished, there wasn't much in it to lose. Pumping it clear again was just about the only setback. They had been the lucky ones.

As the neighborhood began rebuilding, there were more and more reports of places that wouldn't be coming back for a long time, if at all. In the midst of all the negative news, the Dead Rabbit kept up its plans to open.

For those who lived and worked in the neighborhood, whose day-to-day lives had been turned upside down by the storm, the reports of the Dead Rabbit's imminent arrival were some of the only good news available. For some, it became a beacon of hope for the neighborhood. The Dead Rabbit would become the first new bar and restaurant to open in the neighborhood after the storm.

Despite the historic status of the building's façade, the interior at 30 Water Street had been neglected for most of its existence. What many guests fail to realize today is that the Dead Rabbit is an act of creation, not preservation. Every 1850s detail in its woodwork or décor that one sees today was placed there during construction and outfitting between 2012 and 2013. All except the gorgeous, original beams that hold the ceilings. Elegant hulks of timber like that aren't made anymore, and Danny made certain that they were appropriately showcased with a series of tiny spotlights in the Parlor.

The walls were decked with vintage prints, uniforms worn by the bartenders were based on the gang's red flannel shirt and grey checkered trousers, and the glassware and chinaware was selected with great care to reflect the period. Every detail about the presentation had to be perfect. And so it was.

And what would this perfect vessel contain? A revolutionary return to another era of convivial drinking. From Jack's sheaves of notes, after months of exhaustive testing and reformulation, would come the 72 mixed drinks available at the Dead Rabbit's opening—only a couple of years behind schedule—on February 12, 2013, the anniversary of the birth of both Abraham Lincoln and John "Old Smoke" Morrissey.

TALES OF THE COCKTAIL, 2013

Just five months after the opening of the Dead Rabbit, Sean Muldoon was in New Orleans again in July 2013 for the latest Tales of the Cocktail Spirited Awards ceremony. This time he was joined by his Dead Rabbit partners, and especially Jack McGarry. After not being admitted to the Spirited Awards in 2009 because he was not yet of drinking age in the U.S., Jack was returning four years later as a nominee for International Bartender of the Year.

The Dead Rabbit had been selected to compete in several categories, including World's Best Cocktail Menu, World's Best Drinks Selection, World's Best New Cocktail Bar, as well as Jack's category. Clustered around their ballroom table, Team Dead Rabbit awaited their latest judgment.

When the first category came up, for the menu, well, of course they won. Jack used the award itself, a crystal, engraved dish, to serve shots of Redbreast. Drinks selection was a miss, but winning it wasn't a core desire. After a long period during which other awards were given—the details are lost to time—another Dead Rabbit contender was up. Jack McGarry, the youngest ever nominee for International Bartender of the Year, and only the second (after the legendary Audrey Saunders of the Pegu Club) based in America.

Whenever an award was won in the hall, the winner's hometown team screamed and hollered. But even though they were just one table out of dozens, the Dead Rabbit team seemed to always be the loudest. When Jack won, the cheering went on long and loud. Some of the shouting was directly into Jack's beaming face from the tearful, proud face of Muldoon.

And in the climax of the evening, the Dead Rabbit officially became the best new cocktail bar to open in the past twelve months. Four years earlier, Sean had won his first Tales awards for the Merchant Hotel. Now he had returned with a new bar, in a different city, with an all-new creative concept, and he and Jack had won it all again.

They had set out to be the best. And now they had done it twice. So far.

NOTES ON GLASSWARE

Each drink is paired with its ideal vessel, although it's always possible to get by with what you have at hand. Here are descriptions of the full complement.

❶ COCKTAIL GLASS The standard stemmed glass with a rounded or inverted cone bowl. For our cocktails, the capacity should be modest, 4 to 5 ounces.

❷ PUNCH GLASS This should be a larger version of the cocktail glass, as it will include ice. An 8-ounce glass would be preferred.

❸ TALL GLASS Sometimes called a highball glass, this is a tall, straight-sided glass for long drinks served with ice. Generally 8 to 10 ounces in capacity.

❹ ROCKS GLASS Sometimes called an Old Fashioned glass, this is a less voluminous glass for short drinks served with ice. Generally 6 to 8 ounces in capacity.

❺ CHAMPAGNE FLUTE The standard tall, stemmed flute, of 6 to 8 ounces.

❻ WINE GLASS A small, stemmed red wine glass of 8 ounces.

❼ SHERRY GLASS We suggest the use of 3-ounce sherry glasses for posset, although historically a posset set would be used (check the attic!).

❽ PORCELAIN CUP The Lamb's Wool is hot stuff, so a small porcelain or ceramic cup or mug is probably best.

❾ PUNCH BOWL AND CUPS Have fun with using your own punch bowls and cups, of porcelain or of glass. With punch cups, capacity doesn't matter as much because you can always ladle out more.

❿ IRISH COFFEE GLASS Officially and historically, Irish coffee is served in a 6-ounce, tulip-shaped glass with no handle. Many modern variations of this container exist; just make sure you are using a stemmed glass and not a ceramic mug. If you can't see the contrasting layers of light and dark, the excitement of this drink has been drained long before its glass.

A NOTE ON SPIRITS
AND INGREDIENTS

Only a few years ago, many ingredients for historical cocktails were long defunct and thereby out of the reach of the inquisitive modern drinker. But now, enterprising industrialists and cocktail historians have filled enormous gaps in the alcoholic pharmacopeia. While before an ingredient might have only been a curiosity mentioned in a dusty tome, today one has a choice of purveyors of such arcana as Parfait Amour, Old Tom gin, allspice dram, and dozens of other liqueurs, liquors, and bitters.

However, in the United States and abroad, what you can get largely relates to where you live. Throughout the book we have specified brands of spirit that are used in the recipes the way they have been made at the Dead Rabbit; therefore, for maximum fidelity, the same brand of ingredient should be used. Where that ingredient is unavailable however, feel free to use what is. We must never let the perfect be the enemy of the potable.

NKS

COMMUNAL PUNCH

Installing the cocktail parlor of the Dead Rabbit at the top of a narrow, steep set of creaking, wooden stairs worried Sean a bit. When a patron plummeted all the way down within hours of opening the very first night, he stopped worrying. Its baptism was now past.

Drunk people are actually quite adept at falling without injury, not that this should be considered a tip for amateur parachutists. At Sean's previous roost, the Merchant Hotel in Belfast, many found themselves taking the quicker route down its immense stone steps.

Bowls of punch were often the best method to get there.

Depending on drinking style, the large format of the punch bowl is a fork in the road. One path leads to communal enjoyment of its contents with friends and the soon-to-be friendly. But if you instead choose quality over quantity, you can grab one giant straw and reap all its benefits alone. It also saves the washing of glasses.

At the Merchant, a featured beverage was the legendary Philadelphia Fish House Punch, which we will encounter soon enough in this chapter. Among other delights, it included half a bottle of cognac, a quarter bottle of rum, and a quarter bottle of peach eau de vie, totaling an entire bottle of booze per bowl. Next to the description on the menu were the unhelpful, almost judgmental, words "Serves ten."

A different interpretation was taken by two young women who appeared at the bar early one evening. They were clearly dressed for their big night out, having saved their pennies for weeks to visit Belfast's premier cocktail venue. That they ordered the Fish House Punch for themselves alone was perhaps not shocking—it was evidence of the seriousness with which they took their enjoyment of life. But when they quickly called for a refill, the back bar was embroiled in some controversy. Finally, the decision was made to honor this request, as the young ladies seemed in no great way affected by what they had absorbed so far.

When they finished the second bowl as well, each woman had now consumed the equivalent of an entire bottle of liquor on her own. However, friends, this was Ireland. They were still standing, as proud and jovial as when they arrived. The bar staff admired their fortitude. Moments later, when they took a simultaneous tumble down those stone steps and bounced halfway into the street, they leapt up and laughed like the good sports they were. Not only did they have a battle story to tell their friends in the office the next day, but more importantly we had one for this book.

It is this exciting quality—the sense of adventure and almost inevitable danger to life and limb—which defines that most heroic of beverages, the punch.

The exact origin of punch is lost to time, although just about everything known can be found in David Wondrich's one-volume history, *Punch: The Delights (and Dangers) of the Flowing Bowl.* The good professor has done much unique and important primary source research into the origins of many recipes, research that has served as an inspiration for all of the historical re-creations of Sean and Jack.

What seems clear is that punch is a product of the collision of the European colonial powers with the bounteous exotic agriculture of Asia. It is Asia that gave us the modern staples of citrus, tea, and sugar—plus a peculiar liquor called *arrack.* In Arabic, *arak* refers to any distilled liquor, and, accordingly, in South and Southeast Asia, arrack is made from whatever is on hand, such as coconut, palm, or especially sugarcane. When British sailors arriving in India and points east were served combinations of arrack (sometimes transcribed by them, affectionately, as "rack"), sugar, lime, and tea, word traveled fast back home about this new style of Indian drink. Fortunately, arrack is once again available to us today, and is seized upon in one of the following punches.

Far from the garishly colored artificial fruit and ginger ale concoctions that would be punch's pale echo in the twentieth century, the original punch was a milestone in European drinking culture. Punch was immediately welcomed in Europe in the 1600s as a noble conqueror in much the way that Europeans in Asia were not.

MERITON LATROON'S BANTAM PUNCH

Inspiration: Richard Head/Francis Kirkman, *The English Rogue, Continued, in the Life of Meriton Latroon and Other Extravagants. Comprehending the Most Eminent Cheats of Most Trades and Professions. The Second Part*, 1668

An early mention of punch in English literature comes from *The English Rogue: Described in the Life of Meriton Latroon, a Witty Extravagant*, authored in 1665 by Richard Head. Its antihero spends so much time stealing, seducing, and swilling that he is banished from England. Perhaps this plays into his hand, for in the city of Bantam, on the Indonesian island of Java, he discovers a new hobby in the drinking "very immoderately of punch, rack, tea &c." It's not until a second volume, seemingly written by Head's publisher Francis Kirkman without the original author's involvement, that an actual recipe is mentioned, however:

"I had a full enjoyment of every thing the Country afforded: for we had not only the Country drink called *Toddee*, which is made from the juyce of several Trees, and *Punch* which is made of Rack-lime, or lime-water, Sugar, Spices, and sometimes the addition of *Amber-greese* . . ."

Leaving this early mention of "toddy" to one side, let us untangle the recipe for the punch. From the context, the author seems not to know what "rack" refers to, conflating it with lime to suggest lime juice, rather than a type of alcohol. So we'll separate those both back into ingredients we understand. Then there is the inclusion of ambergris, grey amber, "amber grease"—an exotic ingredient indeed, being a blob of fat from the intestines of a sperm whale that has bobbed along in the brine until its original gastric scent has mellowed and matured into something richly floral. Until synthetics and the Endangered Species Act overtook it, ambergris was a significant component of perfumes. As Herman Melville noted in a chapter of *Moby-Dick* dedicated to the substance, "Who would think, then, that such fine ladies and gentlemen should regale themselves with an essence found in the inglorious bowels of a sick whale!"

Jack wanted to make this punch without delving into the bowels of a whale or violating federal law, so this is our updated recipe, fat-free and vegan-friendly.

Without the overly perfumed aspect of ambergris, the drink becomes light and zesty. In fact, this is the lightest of all our communal punches, but yet has a funky undercurrent to it due to the character of arrack. This punch would be appropriate for anyone who likes Daiquiris, Caipirinhas, or Mojitos.

+ Prepare an oleo-saccharum (see below) with the lime peels and sugar.

+ Combine the oleo-saccharum with all the other ingredients, except the garnish, in a large mixing bowl and stir until the sugar has dissolved.

+ Strain through a chinois into a punch bowl. Place a large block of ice in the bowl.

+ To serve, add a small chunk of ice to each cup. Garnish with freshly grated nutmeg.

YIELDS *About 8 Servings*

8 limes

2 cups granulated sugar

25 ounces Batavia Arrack Van Oosten

25 ounces Earl Grey tea, cold

1 cup coconut palm sugar

6½ ounces fresh lime juice

Fresh nutmeg, grated, for garnish

OLEO-SACCHARUM

+ Oleo-saccharum (or sugared oil) is the secret of great punch. Much of the flavor of citrus is locked up in the oil contained in its skin, not its juice. This simple process gets it out.

+ Peel each lime, being sure to remove only the peel, with none of the white pith. A Microplane grater or vegetable peeler is best.

+ Add the peels to a bowl, along with the sugar. Using a muddler or heavy wooden spoon, press the peels into the sugar. You will see oil from the peels collect in the bowl. Let the combination sit for at least 30 minutes at room temperature. Mix to collect all separated oil into the sugar before using.

+ You may use the peeled limes for juicing as needed in the recipe above.

CAPTAIN RADCLIFFE'S PUNCH

Inspiration: Alexander Radcliffe, "Bacchinalia Coelestia, or a Poem in Praise of Punch," 1680

In the seventeenth century, arrack's drawback as a basis for punch was that you had to go to Asia to get it. As punch's popularity surged in Europe and its American colonies, local substitutes were found: brandy in Europe and Caribbean rum in America. However, for the upper classes, nothing on the menu could compare to wine of the grape, with its multifaceted possibilities of flavor. So, fashionable punch had to include it, and Punch Royal was created.

In Radcliffe's original, a recipe in verse form, each of the Greek gods offers up an ingredient in keeping with his or her jurisdiction. An example of the work:

BACCHUS gave notice by dangling a Bunch,
That without his Assistance there could be no Punch

Words to live by. So we have Bacchus himself to thank for a new ingredient in punch: wine. Specifically, French dessert wine. Jack decided to take a strong stand here against the overly sweet reputation of punch—a reputation sometimes unmerited, but troubling nonetheless—by removing not only the dessert wine from this recipe but indeed the sugar. Instead, he has cast a wine-based quinine aperitif and raspberry cordial in those roles.

The result is the fruitiest of our communal punches, concentrated on the tannic and bitter pairing of Byrrh and Ceylon (backed with the quinine tincture) with the under-note of raspberry (backed with rose water). Though we risk the anger of the gods in changing their recipe, we do it all for you.

DIRECTIONS

+ Combine all the ingredients, except the garnish, in a large mixing bowl.

+ Strain through a chinois into a punch bowl. Place a large block of ice in the bowl.

+ To serve, add a small chunk of ice to each cup. Garnish with freshly grated nutmeg.

YIELDS *12 Servings*

INGREDIENTS

10 ounces Raspberry Cordial (see recipe below)

10 dashes Quinine Tincture (see recipe at right)

10 ounces fresh lemon juice

10 ounces framboise eau de vie

10 ounces Byrrh Grand Quinquina

10 ounces Rémy Martin 1738 Cognac

25 ounces Ceylon tea, cold

5 drops rose water

Fresh nutmeg, grated, for garnish

RASPBERRY CORDIAL

+ Purée the raspberries in a blender until smooth. Pour the purée into a small mixing bowl and add the sugar syrup. Stir to combine well.

+ Strain through a chinois into a bottle. Use a spoon to press as much liquid from the solids as possible.

+ Add the rose water and Everclear to the bottle and shake to mix. It will keep for 2 to 3 weeks in the refrigerator.

YIELDS *About 18 ounces*

3 ounces raspberries

16 ounces Sugar Syrup (see recipe at right)

½ ounce rose water

½ ounce Everclear

SUGAR SYRUP

+ Combine the sugar and water in a small saucepan over medium heat, but do not boil. Slowly stir to dissolve the sugar. When the syrup has thickened, remove from the heat. Use a funnel to pour into bottles. The syrup will keep for 2 to 3 weeks in the refrigerator.

YIELDS *About 20 ounces*

2 cups granulated sugar

2 cups water

QUININE TINCTURE

+ Combine the cinchona bark and Everclear in a jar. Allow to macerate for 3 days, then strain through a chinois into a fresh container. Add the water. Due to the alcohol content, this tincture should last indefinitely at room temperature.

YIELDS *About 10 ounces*

1 ounce powdered cinchona bark

4½ ounces Everclear

4½ ounces water

PHILADELPHIA FISH HOUSE PUNCH

Inspiration: Jerry Thomas, *The Bar-Tender's Guide*, 1862

As previously stated, both rum- and brandy-based punches had their day in their respective hemispheres. But by the early nineteenth century, brandy and rum (both imported, of course) were found together as the foundation for the latest British punch recipes.

The types of rum available then were also different to what we know today. Even though the last decade has brought many once-abandoned ingredients and products back onto the bartender's shelves—largely through the efforts of a few committed producers with a historical bent—one significant historical rum has yet to be fully revived, and that is the "London dock" style of dark Jamaican rum. In this style, a funkier, grassy note merges with the molasses. Jack's approach is to create a modern-day stand-in through the combination of three modern rums: Smith & Cross, Banks 7, and Cruzan Blackstrap. Each contributes elements of the historical profile.

Many beloved drink recipes originate in the hallowed halls of social clubs, for which they must have been a unique selling proposition for new members and a comfort to existing ones. One of the world's longest-running clubs, and one of its most mysterious, is the Schuylkill Fishing Company of Pennsylvania, established in 1732.

The grandees of the day organized their club on land let to them by the Lenape tribe, and thus considered it "the Colony in Schuylkill" in equivalence with the better-known thirteen. (History does not retain why the colony should be "in" rather than "of," but this is the kind of quirkery that private clubs seem to revel in.) After independence, they updated to "the State in Schuylkill" but continued their peculiar practices, the most significant being Fish House Punch. In that case at least, the secret is apparently out.

This punch was traditionally made in the same bowl used for baptizing the members' children, underscoring the importance of both practices. Its base was the usual lemon juice, sugar, rum, and cognac. At its crux was the colonial staple: peach brandy, meaning brandy made from peaches, not just grape brandy flavored in that way. Peach brandy did not survive Prohibition, and was unavailable for years, but is on the market again.

Due to the long-missing ingredient, the punch has achieved a kind of mythic stature among the cognoscenti. Now we can make it again, but let's make it our way, with a heightened herbal cast in honor of those hunting and fishing parties who ventured out into the Pennsylvania wilderness.

Perhaps the recent revival of speakeasies, hidden behind revolving doors in blind alleyways and requiring the secret password, fill a need for a kind of contemporary version of the members' club, a bit exclusive yet disposable. There are no dues to pay, so you can try another one tomorrow night. We'd like to think that the next stage, where hospitality and conviviality can shine without the need of exclusionary gimmickry, is embodied by projects like the Dead Rabbit. And get rid of the secret knocks; if the drinks are good, let everyone try them.

Punch was the first category listed in the menus of both the Merchant and the Dead Rabbit, and part of that focus comes from the celebratory nature of punch, its reverent presentation in shining bowls like an offering to the gods. At the Merchant Hotel, silver punch bowls would be delivered on a special trolley and meted out to guests' cups by ladle as they oohed and aahed. Every detail of this service had been thought through, in fitting with punch's history and the five-star nature of the Merchant. Every detail, Sean admits, with one exception—the punches didn't taste very good.

That somewhat important aspect was corrected at the Dead Rabbit. The same pomp and ceremony surrounds the unveiling of the punch bowl (decorated porcelain this time, with non-matching teacups) but we hope you'll agree the recipes are delicious. The Fish House Punch explained above is the Dead Rabbit version. We invite the aforementioned punch-fancying ladies from Belfast to try this version when they have the chance.

A note on "sherbet": In this and other recipes, we use "sherbet" in its British sense as it would have been understood at the time of these historical sources— a rich, flavored syrup. It should not be confused with ice cream or sorbet. However, don't worry, there's a drink with that ingredient coming up, too.

* Combine all the ingredients, except the garnish, in a large mixing bowl.

* Strain through a chinois into a punch bowl. Place a large block of ice in the bowl.

* To serve, add a small chunk of ice to each cup. Garnish with freshly grated nutmeg.

YIELDS *10 Servings*

5 ounces Lemon Sherbet (see recipe below)

10 ounces Laird's Applejack Bonded Proof

3½ ounces Smith & Cross Jamaican Rum

3½ ounces Banks 7 Rum

3 ounces Cruzan Blackstrap Rum

5 ounces Merlet Crème de Pêche

7½ ounces fresh lemon juice

⅓ ounce Dead Rabbit Orinoco Bitters or Angostura Aromatic Bitters

Fresh nutmeg, grated, for garnish

LEMON SHERBET

* Prepare an oleo-saccharum with the lemon peels and sugar (see page 64).

* In a small saucepan, combine the oleo-saccharum and lemon juice over medium heat, but do not boil. Slowly stir to dissolve the sugar. When the syrup has thickened, remove from the heat. Strain through a chinois into bottles. The sherbet will keep for 2 to 3 weeks in the refrigerator.

YIELDS *About 24 ounces*

4 lemons

1½ cups granulated sugar

12 ounces fresh lemon juice

G. M. GURTON'S PUNCH

Inspiration: William Terrington, *Cooling Cups and Dainty Drinks*, 1869

Many of the characters figuring into the creation of historical cocktails are mysterious, with little left behind them in the way of records. Mr. Gurton makes two appearances in William Terrington's 1869 manual, *Cooling Cups and Dainty Drinks*, before disappearing, first to recommend his preferred ingredients in a wine cup (plenty of sugar, citrus, and brandy), and then to detail his punch (plenty of sugar, citrus, and brandy). Jack refocused this recipe by replacing the curaçao in the original with sherry, for a drier, more savory character. In the same vein, ginger extract (available at natural food stores) is preferred to ginger syrup.

With the interaction of lime, green tea, and ginger, there is an exotic quality to this punch. You can introduce it to neophytes as a big brother to the Dark and Stormy.

DIRECTIONS

+ Prepare an oleo-saccharum with the lime peels and granulated sugar (see page 64).

+ Combine the oleo-saccharum with all the other ingredients, except the garnish, in a large mixing bowl and stir until the sugar has dissolved.

+ Strain through a chinois into a punch bowl. Place a large block of ice in the bowl.

+ To serve, add a small chunk of ice to each cup. Garnish with freshly grated nutmeg.

YIELDS *8 Servings*

INGREDIENTS

8 limes

2 cups granulated sugar

1 cup turbinado sugar

2 ounces ginger extract

10 ounces fresh lime juice

10 ounces Rémy Martin 1738 Cognac

6½ ounces oloroso sherry

3¾ ounces Smith & Cross Jamaican Rum

3¾ ounces Banks 7 Rum

2¾ ounces Cruzan Blackstrap Rum

25 ounces green tea, cold

Fresh nutmeg, grated, for garnish

PUNCH À LA TAYLOR

Inspiration: William Terrington, *Cooling Cups and Dainty Drinks*, 1869

This drink has the most complicated flavor of all our punches. In Terrington's original recipe, orange and tamarind lie down with whiskey, which was the basis for this expanded version. We're recommending the strong backbone of Redbreast's pot-stilled flavor.

Pot still whiskey has a hearty cereal character that almost feels nourishing, giving it a heft and touch of funk not seen in typical Irish blends. Using it at cask strength (the alcohol by volume that the whiskey retains straight from the barrel before dilution) adds further fuel to this fire.

Remember that before the 1960s, there were no blended Irish whiskeys, only pot still styles. We're fortunate that Irish producers are now putting emphasis into single pot still styles again, as they really stand up for themselves in mixed drinks.

The herbal notes are Jack's own touches, and as usual he prefers his punch bowls to include tea. This is a good tip for the thrifty as well as the thirsty: any old teacup can contain tea, but with these punches, they will contain tea *and* booze.

There's an idea that punch generally needs to be watered down in order not to knock out imbibers immediately; punch is for marathoners, after all. But Jack doesn't believe in adding an ingredient that isn't also adding a flavor. Why add water when you can add tea? In the same way, why add sugar syrup when you can add tamarind nectar? You'll see this same structure in the other drinks as well.

DIRECTIONS

+ Prepare an oleo-saccharum with the clementine and lemon peels and granulated sugar (see page 64).

+ Combine the oleo-saccharum with all the other ingredients, except the garnish, in a large mixing bowl and stir until the sugar has dissolved.

+ Strain through a chinois into a punch bowl. Place a large block of ice in the bowl.

+ To serve, add a small chunk of ice to each cup. Garnish with freshly grated nutmeg.

YIELDS *10 Servings*

INGREDIENTS

8 clementines

8 lemons

4 cups granulated sugar

10 dashes Eucalyptus Tincture (see recipe below)

6¾ ounces fresh lemon juice

6¾ ounces fresh clementine juice

1 cup turbinado sugar

1 ounce tamarind nectar

2 ounces Suze Gentiane

25 ounces Redbreast 12 Year Old Irish Whiskey

25 ounces Assam tea, cold

15 dashes Dead Rabbit Orinoco Bitters or Angostura Aromatic Bitters

Fresh nutmeg, grated, for garnish

EUCALYPTUS TINCTURE

+ Combine the eucalyptus and Everclear in a jar. Allow to macerate for 3 days, then strain through a chinois into a fresh container. Add the water. Due to the alcohol content, this tincture should last indefinitely at room temperature.

YIELDS *About 10 ounces*

1 ounce dried eucalyptus leaf

4½ ounces Everclear

4½ ounces water

GRANDEUR PUNCH

Inspiration: Harry Johnson, *Bartenders' Manual*, 1888

While your teacups are out, let's move on to a punch truly deserving of its name. Grandeur Punch is a refreshing but elegant exemplar of true punchiness. In the twentieth century, a flavor analogue might be the Southside or Mojito, but let's investigate their punch antecedent.

In fact, the original 1888 recipe takes quite a different path. As "Prussian Grandeur Punch" it celebrated the ascendancy not just of Bismarck but also kümmel, kirschwasser, and brantwein. Well, let's swap Deutsch for Dutch, basing this punch on malty genever, gin's tough old daddy. From there a few changes cascade to keep things in balance. Jack is on top of it, and the grandeur remains.

DIRECTIONS

+ Prepare an oleo-saccharum with the lemon peels and granulated sugar (see page 64).

+ Combine the oleo-saccharum with all the other ingredients, except the garnish, in a large mixing bowl and stir until the sugar has dissolved.

+ Strain through a chinois into a punch bowl. Place a large block of ice in the bowl.

+ To serve, add a small chunk of ice to each cup. Garnish with freshly grated nutmeg.

YIELDS *8 Servings*

INGREDIENTS

8 lemons

2 cups granulated sugar

10 dashes Mace Tincture (see recipe at right)

1¼ cups superfine sugar

9 ounces fresh lemon juice

25 ounces peppermint tea, cold

25 ounces Bols Genever

2 ounces Varnelli l'Anice Secco Speciale

5 dashes Peychaud Bitters

5 dashes Pernod Absinthe

Fresh nutmeg, grated, for garnish

MACE TINCTURE

✦ Combine the mace and Everclear in a jar. Allow to macerate for 3 days, then strain through a chinois into a fresh container. Add the water. Due to the alcohol content, this tincture should last indefinitely at room temperature.

1 ounce dried, pulverized mace

4½ ounces Everclear

4½ ounces water

YIELDS *About 10 ounces*

PISCO PUNCH

Inspiration: William T. Boothby, *The World's Drinks and How to Mix Them*, 1908

The World's Drinks and How to Mix Them was the literary effort of Hon. William "Cocktail" Boothby, Premier Mixologist, sincerely dedicated on its initial page "to the liquor dealers of San Francisco, [w]ho unanimously assisted in my election to the legislature by an unprecedented majority." And until we achieve a new generation of legislators proudly inserting "Cocktail" into their names, it is this volume we must rely on.

In many ways it's a typical bartenders' manual of its time, with helpful suggestions along the lines that rum punch is made like St. Croix rum punch but with rum not from St. Croix, and its recipe for pisco punch is similarly utilitarian: pisco and lemonade and ice. Surely that requires an adjustment by the hand of McGarry.

The South American grape brandy was popular in San Francisco in the Gold Rush era, but again fell out of favor on our shores for a time. But once again, we have survived this interregnum and the pisco flows again. (Peru and Chile compete for the privilege of being listed as pisco's original home, but that debate will not be broached in this equitable volume.)

Almost like drinking a glass of cloudy Chardonnay, the Pisco Punch offers wine-like notes with its fruit, tannin, and grass characteristics.

❈ DIRECTIONS ❈

✦ Prepare an oleo-saccharum with the lemon peels and granulated sugar (see page 64).

✦ Combine the oleo-saccharum with all the other ingredients, except the garnish, in a large mixing bowl and stir until the sugar has dissolved.

✦ Strain through a chinois into a punch bowl. Place a large block of ice in the bowl.

✦ To serve, add a small chunk of ice to each cup. Garnish with freshly grated nutmeg.

Yields *8 Servings*

❈ INGREDIENTS ❈

8 lemons

2 cups granulated sugar

8 dashes Chamomile Tincture (see page 80)

5 ounces Eau de Thé Syrup (see page 80)

25 ounces Pineapple-Infused Pisco (see page 80)

½ cup superfine sugar

9 ounces fresh lemon juice

25 ounces chamomile tea, cold

15 drops rose water

Fresh nutmeg, grated, for garnish

CHAMOMILE TINCTURE

◆ Combine the chamomile and Everclear in a jar. Allow to macerate for 3 days, then strain through a chinois into a fresh container. Add the water. Due to the alcohol content, this tincture should last indefinitely at room temperature.

1 ounce dried, ground chamomile

4½ ounces Everclear

4½ ounces water

YIELDS *About 10 ounces*

EAU DE THÉ SYRUP

◆ Remove the pan from the heat, cover, and let the fern steep for 15 minutes. Strain through a chinois into a bottle. Add the orange flower water. The syrup will keep for 2 to 3 weeks in the refrigerator.

4 cups water

4 cups granulated sugar

½ ounce maidenhair fern

½ ounce orange flower water

YIELDS *About 32 ounces*

PINEAPPLE-INFUSED PISCO

◆ Place the pineapple chunks in a quart canning jar. Fill the jar with pisco and seal it shut.

◆ After 1 hour, strain the mixture through a chinois into a fresh quart jar. Due to the alcohol content, this infusion should last indefinitely at room temperature.

6 ounces pineapple, chopped

750ml bottle pisco

YIELDS *About 750 ml*

PUNCHES FOR THE BAR USE

Communal punch is harmony, Convivial concord, togetherness—communion. Between eight and twelve friends come together and share. Together they remain seated or decide to spill down the stairs for a change. But sometimes punch is too good for friends. It is then that you find yourself in the realm of individually sized punch in disguise as a regular mixed drink.

The distinction between large format punch in a bowl and individually sized punch in a glass is one determined in the eye of the beholder. At the Dead Rabbit and the Merchant, there were some drinks we recommended to dive into with pals, and some that we determined might work better one at a time. The latter subcategory of punch follows.

Individual punches are termed by William Schmidt in *The Flowing Bowl* as "for the bar use," meaning made at the bar for customers *à la minute* rather than prepared in advance in a punch bowl. What makes a punch work better one way or another? In fact, it's up to you. As bartenders, Sean and Jack were mindful that more people would order an individually-sized drink than a whole punch bowl, but they didn't want those people to miss out on the delicate flavors of punch. Alternately, many drinks can be scaled up and batched punch bowl–style if you know you will be moving a lot of them.

The drinks in this chapter, since they are specifically made with bars in mind, are based on the nineteenth and twentieth century recipes from the cocktail bar's heyday, rather than the ancestral punches of the seventeenth century with which we began in the previous group.

As punch evolved over the decades into its descendants, fixes, sours, daisies, and other beverages we shall meet in following chapters, one ingredient to make a debut was soda water. The added effervescence over the plain water traditionally used in punches was a delight, and gave even the dullest offerings the glamorous veneer of Champagne.

In some of the following recipes, we will suggest that you add the soda water to your shaker after the drink has been shaken, but before it has been strained into the drink. This is a simple way of mixing the soda water throughout the other ingredients, instead of topping off a glass with soda water and leaving it all on the surface.

Look for an even greater variety of sweeteners in these drinks. Because of the extra time it takes to prepare, oleo-saccharum only figures into one of our individual punches. However, the one recipe that does include it is a legendary "lost drink" from the Dead Rabbit menu and well worth the effort at home.

SPIDER

Inspiration: William Terrington, *Cooling Cups and Dainty Drinks*, 1869

Carbonated water first found its way into punches in the 1780s, but by the time of the publication of the recipe for the Garrick Club Punch in 1835, the bubbling thrill of chilled carbonated water made it a must-have ingredient for forward-thinking *ponchiers*. In Terrington's volume, he elucidates a series of gin punch variations with soda water. (In some cases, the national origin of the water is specified.) Jack has sifted out the best aspects of this bunch, including the soda-less punch à la Burroughs, which substitutes tea.

Terrington's original Spider recipe called only for gin, lemonade, a lemon liqueur called citronelle, and ice. You will see how much more is in this Spider's parlor. We've got lemon freshness galore, with lemon juice, lemon sherbet, and the high-end limoncello made by Nardini. Refreshing but dry, the Spider is highly citric but with a subtle herbaceous backdrop. Compare its qualities to the classic Tom Collins.

DIRECTIONS

+ Add all the ingredients, except the soda water and garnish, to a shaker. Fill with ice and shake. Add the soda water to the shaker and strain the mixture into a punch glass with one chunk of cracked ice. Garnish with freshly grated nutmeg.

INGREDIENTS

3 dashes Mace Tincture (see page 77)

½ ounce Lemon Sherbet (see page 71)

2 ounces Green Tea–Infused Tanqueray London Dry Gin (see recipe page 86)

3 dashes Pernod Absinthe

1 ounce fresh lemon juice

1 ounce Nardini Acqua di Cedro

1½ ounces soda water

Fresh nutmeg, grated, for garnish

GREEN TEA–INFUSED TANQUERAY LONDON DRY GIN

✦ Place the tea bags in a quart canning jar. Fill the jar with the gin and seal it shut.

✦ After 1 hour, remove the tea bags. Due to the alcohol content, this infusion should last indefinitely at room temperature.

YIELDS *About 750ml*

2 bags green tea

750ml bottle Tanqueray London Dry Gin

BILLY DAWSON'S PUNCH

Inspiration: William Terrington, *Cooling Cups and Dainty Drinks*, 1869

This drink is unapologetically dark in character and full of rum. So was its namesake Billy (or sometimes Bully) Dawson, a seventeenth-century London thug and gambler who probably otherwise had nothing to do with this punch.

It first appears in 1863's *Cups and Their Customs* as a narrative about a so-named person who makes the best punch because "I do nothing else." Despite our esteem for such life choices, we were more inspired by the Terrington version. We're talking about a brandy and rum punch, but the secret ingredient is beer.

Beer, the favorite drink of England before its later craze for gin, expectedly makes its way into many eighteenth- and nineteenth-century mixed drinks. Porter (thought to be named for its caloric appeal to those who carried heavy burdens through the streets) is a rich, dark style of beer that makes a strong foundation for this concoction.

DIRECTIONS

+ Add all the ingredients, except the garnish, to a shaker. Fill with ice and shake. Strain into a punch glass with one chunk of cracked ice. Garnish with freshly grated nutmeg.

INGREDIENTS

¾ ounce Lemon Sherbet (see page 71)

1½ ounces Louis Royer VSOP Cognac

1 ounce porter

½ ounce Smith & Cross Jamaican Rum

½ ounce Banks 7 Rum

½ ounce Cruzan Blackstrap Rum

1 ounce fresh lemon juice

3 dashes Dead Rabbit Orinoco Bitters or Angostura Aromatic Bitters

Fresh nutmeg, grated, for garnish

GRASSOT

Inspiration: Jerry Thomas, *The Bar-Tender's Guide*, 1862

This punch, as originally described by "M. Grassot, the eminent comedian of the Palais Royal," is the precursor to the modern Sidecar. It's one of the drinks that best exemplifies the transition from the communal punches to punches for the bar use.

Thomas' recipe was later printed word for word in Leo Engel's 1878 book, *American & Other Drinks*, where it first captured Jack's imagination. He has peeled back the layers of history that thickly surround brandy to reveal Remy V, a recent formulation which, unlike brandy, spends no time aging in oak.

This grape eau de vie is the gossamer foundation for the carefully constructed layers of flavor, alternately herbal, fruity, and "other." The latter category describes Parfait Amour, a strange Victorian concoction that can elevate a drink while still managing to taste of soapy bubble gum. But trust us, in drinks that require it, it works.

DIRECTIONS

• Add all the ingredients, except the garnish, to a shaker. Fill with ice and shake. Strain into a punch glass with one chunk of cracked ice. Garnish with freshly grated mace.

INGREDIENTS

2 ounces Rose Hip–Infused Remy V (see recipe at right)

¾ ounce Strawberry Cordial (see recipe at right)

1 ounce fresh lemon juice

½ ounce Pernod Absinthe

½ ounce Marie Brizard Parfait Amour

Fresh mace, grated, for garnish

ROSE HIP–INFUSED REMY V

+ Place the tea bag in a quart canning jar. Fill the jar with the Remy V and seal it shut.

+ After 1 hour, remove the tea bag. Due to the alcohol content, this infusion should last indefinitely at room temperature.

YIELDS *About 750 ml*

1 bag rose hip tea

750ml bottle Remy V

STRAWBERRY CORDIAL

+ Purée the strawberries in a blender until smooth. Pour the purée into a small mixing bowl and add the sugar syrup. Stir to combine well.

+ Strain through a chinois into bottles. Use a spoon to press as much liquid from the solids as possible.

+ Add the rose water and Everclear to the bottle and shake to mix. The cordial will keep for 2 to 3 weeks in the refrigerator.

YIELDS *About 20 ounces*

6 ounces strawberries

16 ounces Sugar Syrup (see page 67)

½ ounce rose water

½ ounce Everclear

GREEN SWIZZLE

Inspiration: "The Green Swizzle of the Tropics [Letter to the editor]," *The Sun* (New York), October 26, 1903, p. 4

Tireless beverage researcher Darcy O'Neil reports that between 1890 and 1962, at least a dozen newspaper accounts stressed that "if you were going on a trip to Barbados, you must have a 'Green Swizzle.'" Yet none of those accounts mentioned what exactly that drink entailed. Suppositions were that it was a classic Caribbean combination of rum, sugar, and lime. But where was the famous green?

The bartending community eventually determined that the green element was provided by crème de menthe (as shown in Trader Vic's *Bartender's Guide*, 1972). Cocktail historian to the stars David Wondrich wondered if the drink had ever existed at all outside of a P. G. Wodehouse story.

Then Mr. O'Neil discovered a *New York Times* article from 1910 that once again celebrated the Green Swizzle, but crucially noted that the ingredient that made the drink green was wormwood bitters. Thus the pieces fell into place. For Jack's version, he's replacing wormwood bitters with absinthe, which traditionally includes wormwood, and its cousin anisette, for a glorious explosion of tongue-buzzing anise and deep, arboreal bitterness. The coup de grâce is the pistachio syrup. Yes, it takes a while longer to make, but you must try it.

For our inspiration for this drink, rather than choose the helpful 1910 article, we prefer a more amusing letter to the editor of *The Sun* in 1903, from another true believer in the Green Swizzle, signing as "Swizzle Stick." Mr. Stick does not just promote the Swizzle as newspapers seemed to never tire of doing, but takes the time to denigrate the efforts of a previous correspondent, "Jerseyman," who had repeatedly written to *The Sun* to praise liquors based on the bountiful produce of New Jersey:

> *What do we care about pear trees and peach trees, or how many there are of them in bloom? Let "Jerseyman" tell us something about the green swizzle, and see if he can make it with applejack. It is made with a swizzle stick. I'll give him that pointer to start with, and if "Jerseyman" has ever twirled one between his palms I need say no more. If he has not, he has something still to live for. . . . The question is whether "Jerseyman" or any of your other drink sharps ever heard of wormwood bitters or Falernum? The combination smacks of the tropical soil of the land of mace and cinnamon and cocoa, and, no doubt, would be as out of place on the banks of the Raritan as a polar bear in the Amazon.*

+ After squeezing limes for juice, reserve half a squeezed lime, which will be used for garnish as a lime shell.

+ Add all the ingredients, except the garnish, to a small mixing bowl. Add cracked ice. Swizzle vigorously with a swizzle stick. Pour the contents into a tall glass, topping off with more ice. Serve with a straw, lime shell, mint sprigs, and a dusting of freshly grated nutmeg.

¾ ounce Pistachio Syrup (see recipe at right)

3 dashes Bay Leaf Tincture (see recipe below)

2½ ounces Rhum JM Blanc

1 ounce fresh lime juice

¼ ounce Marie Brizard Anisette

4 dashes Pernod Absinthe

1 ounce Dry Soda Co. wild lime soda

Mint sprigs, for garnish

Fresh nutmeg, grated, for garnish

Half a squeezed lime, for garnish

BAY LEAF TINCTURE

+ Combine the bay leaf and Everclear in a jar. Allow to macerate for 3 days, then strain through a chinois into a fresh container. Add the water. Due to the alcohol content, this tincture should last indefinitely at room temperature.

YIELDS *About 10 ounces*

1 ounce powdered bay leaf

4½ ounces Everclear

4½ ounces water

PISTACHIO SYRUP

* Place the pistachios in a large mixing bowl and cover with 4 cups of hot water. Allow to sit for 30 minutes, then strain off the water.

* Purée the pistachios in a blender until smooth, adding another 4 cups of hot water. Pour the water and pistachio mixture back into the mixing bowl and allow to sit for 2 hours.

* Strain off the resulting "pistachio milk" into a large saucepan using a chinois. Discard the nut solids.

* Add the sugar to the saucepan over medium heat, but do not boil. Slowly stir until the sugar has dissolved.

* Remove the pan from the heat. Strain through a chinois into bottles. Add the Everclear and orange flower water. The syrup will keep for 2 to 3 weeks in the refrigerator.

YIELDS *About 32 ounces*

8 ounces raw pistachios, shelled

8 cups hot water

4 cups granulated sugar

½ ounce Everclear

Dash orange flower water

BANKER'S PUNCH

Inspiration: Tim Daly, *Daly's Bartenders' Encyclopedia*, 1903

You might consider it an Irish Planter's Punch. This drink is also reminiscent of a better-known beverage of the era, the Knickerbocker, but with the welcome addition of a healthy slug of Irish whiskey. The port and fruit flavors serve to soften the fiery whiskey-and-rum combination for another Dead Rabbit recipe that is balanced like a costumed elephant on a tightrope.

Redbreast single pot still, cask strength whiskey is specified here. (See Punch à la Taylor, page 74, for a description of the pot still character.)

Tim Daly was a meticulously accurate bartender whose recipes still appeal today. He took classics and made them his own. Now we've taken our turn and we hope he doesn't mind.

Daly notes, "[t]his is much sought after by bankers and brokers," but we like it anyway.

✣ DIRECTIONS ✣

+ Add all the ingredients, except the garnish, to a shaker. Fill with ice and shake. Strain into a punch glass with one chunk of cracked ice. Garnish with freshly grated nutmeg.

✣ INGREDIENTS ✣

¾ ounce Raspberry Cordial (see page 66)

¾ ounce fresh lime juice

¾ ounce Graham's Late Bottled Vintage Port

¼ ounce Smith & Cross Jamaican Rum

¼ ounce Banks 7 Rum

¼ ounce Cruzan Blackstrap Rum

¾ ounce Redbreast 12 Year Old Cask Strength Whiskey

3 dashes Dead Rabbit Orinoco Bitters or Angostura Aromatic Bitters

Fresh nutmeg, grated, for garnish

PUNCH À LA ROMAINE

Inspiration: Charles Ranhofer, *The Epicurean: A Complete Treatise of Analytical and Practical Studies on the Culinary Art*, 1893

Ladies and gentlemen, silence, if you please. You are in the presence of greatness. This drink, the Punch à la Romaine, is the one recipe in this volume that you couldn't order at the Dead Rabbit, or even the Merchant Hotel. Yes, it was even on the menu at the Dead Rabbit for an entire year. History tells us that during that period it was served only three times: once to Sean Muldoon and twice to Ben Schaffer because he took one of Sean's. But after that it vanished again. You might say that this drink is not available in any bar, but the bar in which it was first unavailable was the Dead Rabbit.

The reason for Punch à la Romaine's unexcused absence from the Dead Rabbit is that the drink requires a type of ice, a crunchy Italian granita, which is difficult to adapt for bar service. It takes a long time to prepare, it fills a lot of space in the freezer, and it doesn't last long when it comes out.

However, the good news is that none of these problems face you in creating it at home, where you get to decide what your guests (and, more importantly, you yourself) will drink. And if you decide it will be Punch à la Romaine, you will not receive complaints, but you may receive unexpected visits. Especially from Sean Muldoon and Ben Schaffer. (If this occurs, be kind, and let Sean have two this time.)

Essentially, this is a combination of Champagne punch and lemon ice, two delicacies that came of age at the same time in the late eighteenth century. Many books put forth a version of Punch à la Romaine; our recipe is based on that from Charles Ranhofer's enormous tome distilling his thirty years' experience as the chef at Delmonico's, the legendary New York restaurant.

* Pre-chill punch glasses in your freezer.

* Mix the Punch Granita and Italian Meringue Egg Whites together in a small stainless steel or copper bowl with a hand-held blender until puréed. Spoon into a glass. Top with the Champagne. Garnish with freshly grated nutmeg.

4 ounces Punch Granita (see recipe below)

2 tablespoons Italian Meringue Egg Whites (see recipe at right)

2 ounces brut Champagne

Fresh nutmeg, grated, for garnish

PUNCH GRANITA

* Prepare an oleo-saccharum with the lemon peels and sugar (see page 64).

* Combine the oleo-saccharum with all the other ingredients in a large mixing bowl and stir until the sugar has dissolved.

* Strain through a chinois and chill in the freezer for 24 hours.

YIELDS *About 36 ounces*

6 lemons

⅝ cup superfine sugar

4 ounces fresh lemon juice

16 ounces water

6 ounces Smith & Cross Jamaican Rum

6 ounces Banks 7 Rum

5 ounces Cruzan Blackstrap Rum

1 ounce Green Chartreuse

ITALIAN MERINGUE EGG WHITES

* In a small stainless steel or copper mixing bowl, beat the egg whites to stiff peaks.

* Add the sugar and water to a small saucepan and bring to a low boil, stirring frequently. Using a candy thermometer, determine when the mixture has reached between 236° to 238°F.

* At that stage, pour the resulting syrup in a slow, narrow stream into the egg whites, folding it in as you pour. When all the syrup has been added, stir until the mixture is smooth.

YIELDS *About 5 ounces*

2 large egg whites

¾ cup granulated sugar

3 ounces water

SOURS AND FIZZES

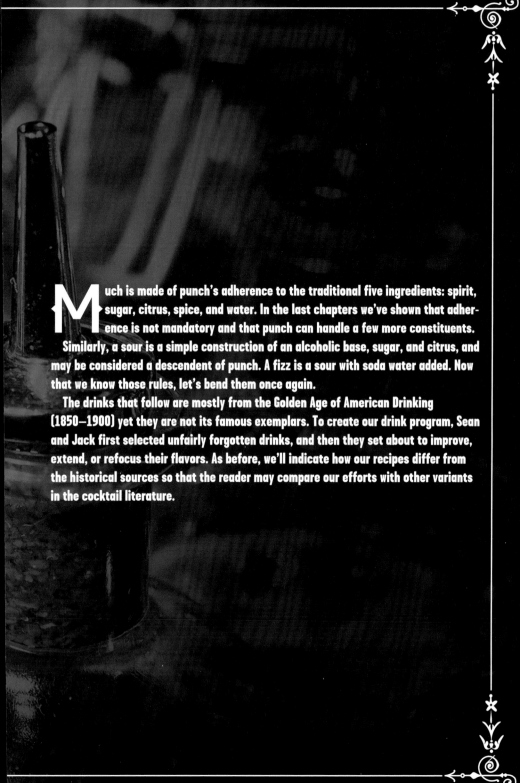

Much is made of punch's adherence to the traditional five ingredients: spirit, sugar, citrus, spice, and water. In the last chapters we've shown that adherence is not mandatory and that punch can handle a few more constituents. Similarly, a sour is a simple construction of an alcoholic base, sugar, and citrus, and may be considered a descendent of punch. A fizz is a sour with soda water added. Now that we know those rules, let's bend them once again.

The drinks that follow are mostly from the Golden Age of American Drinking (1850–1900) yet they are not its famous exemplars. To create our drink program, Sean and Jack first selected unfairly forgotten drinks, and then they set about to improve, extend, or refocus their flavors. As before, we'll indicate how our recipes differ from the historical sources so that the reader may compare our efforts with other variants in the cocktail literature.

MAIDEN'S BLUSH

Inspiration: Louis Fouquet, *Bariana*, 1896

This drink is documented in many a bar guide, first in *Recipes of American and Other Drinks* (Charlie Paul, 1887) where its formulation was the same as in the later *Bariana*: Old Tom gin, absinthe, lemon juice, and raspberry cordial. By the time it appeared in *Barflies and Cocktails* (Harry McElhone, 1927) it had lost its citrus, and this shortcoming was repeated in *The Artistry of Mixing Drinks* (Frank Meier, 1934). In Harry Craddock's *Savoy Cocktail Book* (1930), the lemon juice was back, but the raspberry had turned to grenadine and, more alarmingly for the notion of balance, the biting absinthe had turned to another sweetener, curaçao.

But in 1937, W. J. Tarling published his *Café Royal Cocktail Book*, and the recipe was restored to something resembling its nineteenth-century glory. We salute both Tarling and M. Fouquet, whose delicious versions bookend decades of decline where the Maiden's Blush is concerned.

Our version closely parallels the original recipe, but we feel confident about absinthe and have brought it strongly forward. For the gin component, we recommend Ransom Old Tom, which is an atypical example as it has been barrel-aged, imparting a woody flavor.

This is an adventurous potation, exceedingly complex for a sour. Absinthe figures prominently in many of our drinks, as it was an important and popular ingredient in the era from which we derive our inspiration. The Maiden's Blush is a good introduction to absinthe, to prepare you for drinks yet to come.

⊹ DIRECTIONS ⊹

• Add all the ingredients to a shaker. Fill with ice and shake. Strain into a punch glass.

⊹ INGREDIENTS ⊹

1 ounce Raspberry Cordial (see page 66)

¾ ounce fresh lemon juice

1 ounce Pernod Absinthe

1½ ounces Ransom Old Tom Gin

APPLE BLOSSOM

Inspiration: William Schmidt, *The Flowing Bowl*, 1892

Schmidt's original called for applejack, sugar syrup, and crème de roses. Not as inventive as most of his libations, but it nonetheless put Jack thinking about fruit and flowers coming together in a brandy-based drink.

In this final work, Calvados substitutes its slightly more pungent flavor for American applejack, and the fruit flavors multiply to include strawberry and ruby grapefruit. You could think of it as a cousin to the Sidecar, which would not appear for another generation. In Robert Vermeire's *Cocktails: How to Mix Them* (1922), he notes that the Sidecar "is very popular in France. It was first introduced in London by MacGarry [sic], the celebrated bar-tender of Buck's Club." This adds credence to certain theories of how Jack McGarry learned so much about historical drinks.

⁂DIRECTIONS⁂

✦ Add all the ingredients to a shaker. Fill with ice and shake. Strain into a punch glass.

⁂INGREDIENTS⁂

2 ounces Strawberry-Infused Château du Breuil Calvados (see recipe at right)

½ ounce Strawberry Cordial (see page 89)

1 ounce fresh lemon juice

¾ ounce Combier Pamplemousse Rose

3 dashes Bittermens Hopped Grapefruit Bitters

STRAWBERRY-INFUSED CHÂTEAU DU BREUIL CALVADOS

+ Chop and hull the strawberries. Place the strawberries in a quart canning jar. Fill the jar with Calvados and seal it shut.

+ After 2 hours, strain the mixture through a chinois into a fresh quart jar. Due to the alcohol content, this infusion should last indefinitely at room temperature.

YIELDS *About 750 ml*

½ pound fresh strawberries

750ml bottle Château du Breuil Calvados

PISTACHE FIZZ

Inspiration: George J. Kappeler, *Modern American Drinks*, 1895

The Ramos Gin Fizz, created by Henry Charles Ramos of New Orleans in 1888, is a beloved classic. A kind of elevated gin milkshake, partaking of it has been described as "drinking a flower."

If it was going to celebrate the greatest styles of historical drinking, the Dead Rabbit needed an analogue to the famed Ramos. This variant, first published in Kappeler's guide, came on the scene. If the Ramos version of a Gin Fizz tastes like a flower, why not go further with the greenery, adding leaves and nuts to the petals? Using pistachio as an alternative sweetener brings in its notes of pine and lime. It was a natural progression to bring in lime juice itself instead of the original lemon, and green tea as another herbal leaf.

Unlike many bar operators of his era, Mr. Ramos disclosed his famous recipe during his lifetime—although only after Prohibition had put him out of business.

DIRECTIONS

- Add all the ingredients, except the soda water, to a shaker and shake. Add ice and shake again vigorously for at least a minute. Strain into a tall glass and add the soda water.

INGREDIENTS

3 dashes Eucalyptus Tincture (see page 75)

1 ounce Pistachio Syrup (see page 93)

2½ ounces Green Tea–Infused Tanqueray London Dry Gin (see page 86)

½ large egg white

¾ ounce heavy cream

¾ ounce fresh lime juice

1½ ounces soda water

MORNING REVIVER

Inspiration: Tim Daly, *Daly's Bartenders' Encyclopedia*, 1903

The concept of an alcoholic beverage to undo the ravages of previously consumed alcoholic beverages is a timeless one. In *The Gentleman's Companion* (1939), the esteemed Charles H. Baker collected twenty-seven "Picker-Uppers" designed for this noble task. Baker traveled the world, largely by well-stocked yacht, and reported on all manner of native imbibing for the good of humanity. But he never made it to Belfast, where the Merchant Hotel listed a Baker-beating thirty-seven cures for "the morning after the evening before."

This fizzy number may not cure you, but we're sure it couldn't hurt. In the words of Daly, "When a person awakes in the morning with a desire for a stimulant and does not know what it shall be, the reviver will invariably fill the bill." If you have no idea what you're doing, drink this.

Grande Liqueur de Sapins is a liqueur made from distillation of buds from the pine tree, a bit like an alpine Chartreuse.

You can see many of the ideas already indicated coming together in this drink: tea, absinthe, and flavors of the forest. These are the Jack McGarry touches: learn them well!

DIRECTIONS

✦ Add all the ingredients, except the garnish, to a shaker. Fill with ice and shake. Strain the mixture into an ice-filled tall glass. Garnish with freshly grated nutmeg.

INGREDIENTS

1 ½ ounces Green Tea–Infused Jameson Irish Whiskey (see recipe at right)

¾ ounce Lime Sherbet (see recipe at right)

¼ ounce Pernod Absinthe

¾ ounce fresh lime juice

½ ounce Deniset Klainguer Grande Liqueur de Sapins

1 ounce fresh apple juice

3 dashes Bittermens Boston Bittahs

Fresh nutmeg, grated, for garnish

GREEN TEA–INFUSED JAMESON IRISH WHISKEY

* Place the tea bags in a quart canning jar. Fill the jar with the whiskey and seal it shut.

* After 1 hour, remove the tea bags. Due to the alcohol content, this infusion should last indefinitely at room temperature.

2 bags green tea

750ml bottle Jameson Irish Whiskey

YIELDS *About 750 ml*

LIME SHERBET

* Prepare an oleo-saccharum with the lime peels and sugar (see page 64).

* In a small saucepan over medium heat, combine the oleo-saccharum and lime juice, but do not boil. Slowly stir to dissolve the sugar. When the syrup has thickened, remove from the heat. Strain through a chinois into bottles. The sherbet will keep for 2 to 3 weeks in the refrigerator.

4 limes

1¼ cups granulated sugar

10 ounces fresh lime juice

YIELDS *About 20 ounces*

MEZCAL FIZZ

Inspiration: Charles H. Baker, *The Gentleman's Companion*, 1939

Speaking of Charles Baker, and much of the "smart set" was doing so at one time, here's his own contribution to the annals of tequiliana. Discovering tequila and its brother mezcal at a time when they were unknown to most Americans, Baker nonetheless found the Mexican practice of shooting straight spirit to be wanting. He writes, "We began going on a still hunt for some way to mix tequila. We were greeted with raised eyebrows, expressions of commiseration for waning sanity, open distrust."

After experimentation in his yacht's galley, Baker and his coconspirators concocted the Armillita Chico tequila cocktail, named after "the idol of Mexico, their foremost, most finished, most graceful, most dramatic bull-fighter." A simple tequila sour put together in a blender, it was an inspiration for Jack's innovation, but not as itself ready for prime time.

Here, tequila has been swapped out for smoky mezcal, which is tempered with watermelon juice but reinforced with the brimstone-tinged Bittermens shrub. And it has all been livened with soda water, making Baker's sour into a Dead Rabbit fizz.

DIRECTIONS

+ Add all the ingredients, except the soda and garnish, to a shaker. Fill with ice and shake. Add the soda to the shaker and strain the mixture into an ice-filled tall glass. Garnish with freshly grated nutmeg.

INGREDIENTS

2 ounces Del Maguey Vida Mezcal

¾ ounce grenadine

½ ounce fresh lime juice

1½ ounces watermelon juice

5 dashes Bittermens Hellfire Habanero Shrub

1½ ounces soda water

Fresh nutmeg, grated, for garnish

ALHAMBRA ROYAL

Inspiration: William T. Boothby, *Cocktail Boothby's American Bar-Tender*, 1891

"Many pamphlets heretofore written upon the theme of mixology are absolutely worthless. . . . These so-called guides contain recipes for the mixing of beverages which no practical bartender on earth ever had occasion to serve. The only redeeming features of these decoctions are their high-sounding names, which scheming, imaginative penny-a-liners have given them in order to make large volumes out of little material." So begins William T. "Cocktail" Boothby in the introduction to his volume of recipes. To be sure we understand where he's coming from, he signs off as "Presiding Deity at the famous Hotel Rafael Club House".

Nonetheless, Boothby's recipe for the grandly named Alhambra Royal is: "Pour a pony of cognac into a cup of chocolate and add a little lime juice to it." We chose not to do this.

However, the recipe reminded Jack of the Mulata Daiquiri, which includes crème de cacao. It was popular in Cuba in the 1940s and came to be featured at the Merchant Hotel. Thinking that rum was a more natural fit for the lime and chocolate flavors, this hybrid of 1890s and 1940s was imagined. The patrician name is at no extra charge.

❈DIRECTIONS❈

+ Add all the ingredients to a shaker. Fill with ice and shake. Strain into a punch glass.

❈INGREDIENTS❈

¾ ounce fresh lime juice

½ ounce Varnelli Punch a la Fiamma

¾ ounce Marie Brizard Crème de Cacao

¾ ounce Smith & Cross Jamaican Rum

¾ ounce Banks 7 Rum

½ ounce Cruzan Blackstrap Rum

3 dashes Dead Rabbit Orinoco Bitters or Angostura Aromatic Bitters

PEACH BLOW FIZZ

Inspiration: Hugo Ensslin, *Recipes for Mixed Drinks*, 1916

This is definitely a crowd-pleaser, even though no crowd has yet figured out what the word "peach" is doing in the name, since there's no peach, or what the word "blow" is doing there, for any reason at all. At least we have "fizz" to hang onto.

This recipe hews close to Ensslin's original, with merely the addition of a positively frugal three new flavors.

For commercially available rhubarb soda, you might try the Dry Soda Co. of Seattle. They also make lavender-, vanilla bean-, and cucumber-flavored sodas specified in other recipes in this volume.

·❀DIRECTIONS❀·

✦ Chill a tall glass. Add all the ingredients, except the soda, to a shaker. Fill with ice and shake. Add the soda to the shaker and strain the mixture into the glass.

·❀INGREDIENTS❀·

2 ounces Hibiscus-Infused Tanqueray London Dry Gin (see page 114)

¾ ounce Strawberry Cordial (see page 89)

¼ ounce Merlet Crème de Pêche

½ ounce fresh lime juice

½ ounce fresh lemon juice

¾ ounce heavy cream

1 large egg white

2 dashes Bittermens Burlesque Bitters

1 ounce rhubarb soda

HIBISCUS-INFUSED TANQUERAY LONDON DRY GIN

+ Place the tea bag in a quart canning jar. Fill the jar with the gin and seal it shut.

+ After 1 hour, remove the tea bag. Due to the alcohol content, this infusion should last indefinitely at room temperature.

YIELDS *About 750 ml*

1 bag hibiscus tea

750ml bottle Tanqueray London Dry Gin

LION'S TAIL

Inspiration: William J. Tarling, *Café Royal Cocktail Book*, 1937

If you hadn't already realized this is a different kind of cocktail book, you should by now, because you've come all this way and this is the first drink showcasing bourbon. Bourbon is big these days, so here's a drink to toss to your bourbon-imbibing lions.

You can think of it as a tropical bourbon drink, with its fruit juices and pimento dram. (Pimento, a fruit native to the Greater Antilles and also known as allspice, figures into many of the beverages to come.)

To cause the fruit and spice to play nice together, we're including pear liqueur, and to lasso the nutty bourbon flavor we've added crème de cacao.

DIRECTIONS

* Add all the ingredients, except the garnish, to a shaker. Fill with ice and shake. Strain into a punch glass with one chunk of cracked ice. Garnish with freshly grated nutmeg.

INGREDIENTS

2 ounces Old Forester Bourbon

¾ ounce Crème de Cacao Blanc

¼ ounce Crème de Poire

¼ ounce Pimento Dram

1 ounce fresh lemon juice

¾ ounce orange juice

3 dashes Dead Rabbit Orinoco Bitters or Angostura Aromatic Bitters

Fresh nutmeg, grated, for garnish

MAMIE TAYLOR

Inspiration: Tim Daly, *Daly's Bartenders' Encyclopedia*, 1903

Originally, this evocative name was connected to a straightforward Scotch highball. (Ms. Taylor, like many who have given their name to a mixed drink, was showfolk—an opera singer, in fact.) Here, we've expanded on the basic highball structure to incorporate the McGarry touches: spice, flavored sweeteners, plenty of bitters, and underutilized liqueurs. The creative combination of Strega and Scotch is not obvious, but it is a great stage effect nonetheless. Ring down the curtain.

DIRECTIONS

+ Add all the ingredients, except the soda and garnish, to a shaker. Fill with ice and shake. Add the soda to the shaker and strain the mixture into an ice-filled tall glass. Garnish with freshly grated nutmeg.

INGREDIENTS

¾ ounce Ginger Syrup (see page 118)

3 dashes Mace Tincture (see page 77)

3 dashes Boker's Bitters, or Angostura Aromatic Bitters

¾ ounce fresh lime juice

½ ounce Liquore Strega

2 ounces Great King Street Scotch

1½ ounces soda water

Fresh nutmeg, grated, for garnish

GINGER SYRUP

* Chop the ginger into small pieces and feed them into an automatic juicer. Strain the ginger juice through a chinois to remove the pulp.

* Add the ginger juice, sugar, and water to a large saucepan over medium heat, but do not boil. Slowly stir until the sugar has dissolved.

* Remove the pan from the heat. Use a funnel to pour into bottles. The syrup will keep for 2 to 3 weeks in the refrigerator.

YIELDS *About 750 ml*

12 ounces ginger root

2 cups water

2 cups granulated sugar

WILD IRISH ROSE

Inspiration: Harry Craddock, *The Savoy Cocktail Book*, 1930

Here is a proudly nationalistic take on the classic Jack Rose, improved by complementing its applejack with Connemara Peated Whiskey, an Irish whiskey that tastes like standing on Eire's soil feels.

For our money, pomegranate liqueur and syrup are preferable to industrial grenadine, whose primary ingredient is FD&C Red No. 40. We must also have our bitters and absinthe quotient. And why not some ethereal foam from the white of an egg?

But don't let the soothing foam fool you: The peat makes this Irish rose wild.

❈ DIRECTIONS ❈

✦ Pre-chill a punch glass. Add all the ingredients to a shaker. Fill with ice and shake. Strain into the punch glass.

❈ INGREDIENTS ❈

¾ ounce Pomegranate Syrup (see recipe below)

1 ounce Connemara Peated Single Malt Irish Whiskey

1 ounce Laird's Applejack Bonded Proof

1 ounce Pama Pomegranate Liqueur

¾ ounce fresh lemon juice

3 dashes Bittermens Burlesque Bitters

3 dashes Pernod Absinthe

1 large egg white

POMEGRANATE SYRUP

✦ Add the juice, sugar, and water to a medium saucepan over medium heat, but do not boil. Slowly stir until the sugar has dissolved.

✦ Remove the pan from the heat. Use a funnel to pour into bottles. The syrup will keep for 2 to 3 weeks in the refrigerator.

1 cup pomegranate juice

2 cups granulated sugar

1 cup water

YIELDS *About 16 ounces*

FLORODORA

Inspiration: "Here Is the Latest Drink Inspired by a Chorus Girl,"
The Evening World (New York), July 2, 1901, p. 1

And now, another entry from our favorite category: cocktails whose creation was covered by the daily press. We long for the era in which the headline "Here Is the Latest Drink Inspired by a Chorus Girl" belonged proudly on the front page of a newspaper. (To our fellow cocktail chroniclers, how about a book of *all* the drinks inspired by chorus girls?)

The recipe for this variation of a Gin Buck (a basic gin and ginger ale) was accorded front-page status perhaps for its cooling properties. In the first week of July 1901, New York was in the middle of a record heat wave, and the front page was given over to all aspects of this crisis. Above the recipe, *The Evening World* kept track of the mounting deaths in a column of figures adding up to 260 in one week. Nothing to make light of, yet still the recipe offered its respite.

The chorus girl in question was from the hit show *Florodora*, a bit of frippery whose fame owed much to that girl and her cohorts—the "Florodora girls" as they became known, a term which still echoes in our cultural hallways, however faintly. As the *Evening World* notes, a crowd of actors went to a bar, among them a *Florodora* maiden. While everyone enjoyed spirited beverages, the maiden demurred, saying she had had them all before.

The barman, "Jimmy O'Brien, the head inventor of drinks, was called. He thought until the noise of his thinking drowned the electric fans."

The result was the Florodora. For this reconfiguration, our head inventor of drinks contributed more herbs, more spice, and more bitters, and adjusted the air conditioning while he did it. More, more, more, like the audiences screamed at the end of *Florodora*'s final act.

In *Imbibe!*, David Wondrich muses, "Alas, the article was silent as to which of the pretty maidens it was"—but he need dream in vain no longer. Humbled as we are at the rare opportunity to scoop Wondrich, we must direct him to *The Evening World* of July 3, 1901, page 3, which offers a poem memorializing the "Girl and the New Summer Drink Made in Her Honor: Miss Drake Was the First to Partake of 'The Florodora.'" A sample:

> *Oh, siren of the summer drinks!*
> *A pale rose in the shattered ice*
> *Glows like the cheek of that sweet minx*
> *Who names this drink of paradise.*

Of raspberries their syrup soul
From tender fruit most tender nursed,
And fragrant limes that reach the goal
And make a blessing of a thirst.
Oh, don't forget the Plymouth gin
That makes of water merry jest—
Its pale and weak and soulless twin
That never stirred my lady's breast.

That sort of thing goes on for a few more stanzas before the payoff:

To you, sweet "Florodora" maid,
Who caused this summer blessing's make,
I drink the tipple in the shade
And bless you for it, Susie Drake.

Thank you, Susie Drake, for your commitment to inspiring barmen and newspapermen alike.

❄DIRECTIONS❄

* Add all the ingredients, except the ginger ale and garnish, to a shaker. Fill with ice and shake. Add the ginger ale to the shaker and strain the mixture into an ice-filled tall glass. Garnish with freshly grated nutmeg.

❄INGREDIENTS❄

2 ounces Hibiscus-Infused Tanqueray London Dry Gin (see page 114)

¾ ounce Ginger Syrup (see page 118)

½ ounce Merlet Crème de Framboise

¾ ounce fresh lime juice

3 dashes Bittermens Burlesque Bitters

2 ounces Blenheim Ginger Ale

Fresh nutmeg, grated, for garnish

LALLA ROOKH

Inspiration: George J. Kappeler, *Modern American Drinks*, 1895

Lalla Rookh is the name of a play in poetry and prose written by Thomas Moore and published in 1817. The title means "tulip cheeked" in Persian and is a favorite term of endearment in the romantic poetry of that language. A series of operatic adaptations of Moore's work throughout the nineteenth century kept the name current, and as we've already seen with the Florodora and Mamie Taylor, bartenders and show biz go hand in hand.

Kappeler was the first to publish a recipe for this drink, a sweet dairy hit he concocted from brandy, rum, sugar, cream, and vanilla cordial. Feeding those specs into the bartending computer that doubles as Jack McGarry's brain resulted in a lighter, more balanced recipe. Few people want to drink cream-based drinks all night. But by turning this into a fizz with some flavored soda, the stomach is lifted of its heavy burden even as the taste buds are lifted to frothing heights.

DIRECTIONS

* Pre-chill a tall glass. Add all the ingredients, except the soda and garnish, to a shaker. Fill with ice and shake. Strain into the tall glass. Add the soda and garnish with freshly grated nutmeg.

INGREDIENTS

1 dash Allspice Tincture (see recipe at right)

1 ounce Vanilla Syrup (see recipe at right)

1 ounce Ron Zacapa Rum

1 ounce Rémy Martin VS Cognac

¾ ounce fresh lime juice

¾ ounce heavy cream

1 large egg white

4 dashes Dead Rabbit Orinoco Bitters or Angostura Aromatic Bitters

1½ ounces vanilla soda

Fresh nutmeg, grated, for garnish

ALLSPICE TINCTURE

+ Combine the allspice and Everclear in a jar. Allow to macerate for 3 days, then strain through a chinois into a fresh container. Add the water. Due to the alcohol content, this tincture should last indefinitely at room temperature.

1 ounce ground allspice
4½ ounces Everclear
4½ ounces water

YIELDS *About 10 ounces*

VANILLA SYRUP

+ Use a paring knife to cut down the center of the vanilla bean pod, being careful to cut through only the top half and not all the way through the pod.

+ Open the pod and scrape the vanilla seeds out with the edge of your knife.

+ Add the seeds, sugar, and water to a large saucepan over medium heat, but do not boil. Slowly stir until the sugar has dissolved.

+ Remove the pan from the heat, cover, and let the seeds steep for 15 minutes. Strain through a chinois into bottles. The syrup will keep for 2 to 3 weeks in the refrigerator.

1 vanilla bean pod
2 cups granulated sugar
2 cups water

YIELDS *About 16 ounces*

STRAITS SLING

Inspiration: Robert Vermeire, *Cocktails and How to Mix Them*, 1922

As tropical drink researcher Jeff "Beachbum" Berry casually understates in his 2010 book *Beachbum Berry Remixed*, "the Singapore Sling has taken a lot of abuse over the years." Like many of the exotically colored mixed drinks evoking foreign ports of call, they were in style, and then they were not. Of course, what matters to us is not changing fashions, but whether it tasted any good. The Singapore Sling, like the Mai Tai, is one of those drinks where bartenders and the populace seem to like the name more than they like faithfully reproducing its actual ingredients. Nowadays you'll often find both drowning in pineapple juice, which was never part of the plan.

Before there was the Singapore Sling, there was the Straits Sling, probably originating not long before its publication in Vermeire's volume. Within a few years, however, the Straits Sling had transmogrified into the Singapore version, with the substitution of sweet cherry brandy for dry cherry eau de vie (otherwise known as kirsch).

For our version? We don't want it to be too sweet or too dry, so let's use a bit of both. We can catch up for the lost richness of the missing portion of brandy with luxurious lemon sherbet and the heady notes of genever instead of the usual gin. As always, flavored soda is preferred to the plain stuff, because we only have so much time to spend on this planet.

·❦DIRECTIONS❦·

✦ Add all the ingredients, except the soda and garnish, to a shaker. Fill with ice and shake. Strain into an ice-filled tall glass. Add the soda and garnish with freshly grated nutmeg.

·❦INGREDIENTS❦·

½ ounce Lemon Sherbet (see page 71)

1½ ounces Bols Genever

½ ounce Cherry Heering

½ ounce Benedictine

½ ounce kirsch eau de vie

¾ ounce fresh lemon juice

3 dashes Dead Rabbit Orinoco Bitters or Angostura Aromatic Bitters

1½ ounces rhubarb soda

Fresh nutmeg, grated, for garnish

DELICIOUS SOUR

Inspiration: William Schmidt, *The Flowing Bowl*, 1892

After all those delicious recipes, it's time for something self-consciously delicious. This is an excellent drink, far preferable to the Disgusting Sour or the Yesterday's Garbage Smash.

Schmidt shows us the way here in his usual high style, delineating a lovely combination of apples, peaches, and limes. Despite it being called a sour and not a fizz, he does insert a squirt of soda water, but we've unsquirted it. Instead, froth comes from an egg white.

However, in the face of all those bright fruit flavors, let's mellow things out with our old favorites: pistachio syrup and eucalyptus tincture. It all comes together to live up to its name, both delicious and sour, just like life.

DIRECTIONS

* Add all the ingredients, except the garnish, to a shaker. Fill with ice and shake. Strain into a punch glass with one chunk of cracked ice. Garnish with freshly grated nutmeg.

INGREDIENTS

3 dashes Eucalyptus Tincture (see page 75)

½ ounce Pistachio Syrup (see page 93)

2 ounces Laird's Applejack Bonded Proof

¼ ounce Merlet Crème de Pêche

¾ ounce fresh lime juice

3 dashes Pernod Absinthe

1 large egg white

Fresh nutmeg, grated, for garnish

The daisy started life as a specialized sour with a hint of orange cordial, as described in the 1876 revision to Jerry Thomas' bar guide. Shortly before 1900, it went pink. Raspberry syrup or grenadine, and increasing amounts of them, were specified in recipes all the way through the 1940s. Jack has staunched this red tide; instead of leaning too heavily on the bright red bottle, our daisies will feature all manner of accents—herbal, floral, or even dark and dry.

A fix is a more ancient beast, prized for its plumage made of pineapple syrup instead of orange or raspberry. As you can see, American bartenders of this era adopted incredibly specific categories for drinks. It must have helped greatly with the accelerated pace of urban life to be able to yell out to the man behind the stick, "Whiskey Fix!" or "Whiskey Daisy!" and not have to waste time specifying the flavor of syrup you expected in your whiskey sour.

The below examples encompass the era of the daisy and fix from approximate start until the styles faded from popular parlance. Rejoice, for they have returned.

For the most part, we have specified that this category be served in punch glasses, our name for a larger cocktail glass. However, at the Dead Rabbit, daisies with ice in them are actually served in "mustache cups." These are large porcelain teacups with a small barrier near the rim, shaped rather like a gentleman's upper lip. This invention prevents hot, wet tea from melting the wax on a carefully prepared mustache, allowing a gentleman to sip without fear.

Even though primly waxed mustaches may be making a comeback among exactly the kind of people who want to drink in bars inspired by the 1850s, the mustache cup's rollout at the Dead Rabbit was for a different, but equally clever reason. Jack found that the 'stache guard worked just as well in preventing ice from hitting the imbiber in the face, allowing an iced drink to be enjoyed in an unusually straw-free experience.

In short: If you have one of these Victorian antiques, now is the time to break it out.

GINGER DAISY

Inspiration: O. H. Byron, *The Modern Bartenders' Guide or Fancy Drinks and How to Mix Them*, 1884

The original called for ginger ale, but we prefer a fresh ginger syrup in concert with vanilla soda. Byron also specified brandy in his version, all of which makes for a nice combination, but we have a brandy daisy coming up next. So for the ginger creation, we're going with equal parts dark rum and redolent sherry, raising the proceedings to another level. Feel the rich molasses and piquant oloroso knit this recipe together.

DIRECTIONS

✦ Add all the ingredients, except the soda and garnish, to a shaker. Fill with ice and shake. Add the soda to the shaker and strain the mixture into a punch glass with one chunk of cracked ice. Garnish with freshly grated nutmeg.

INGREDIENTS

1½ ounces Hop-Infused Gosling's Dark Rum (see page 132)

¾ ounce Ginger Syrup (see page 118)

2 dashes Dead Rabbit Orinoco Bitters or Angostura Aromatic Bitters

¾ ounce fresh lime juice

1½ ounces Barbadillo "San Rafael" Oloroso Sherry

1 ounce vanilla bean soda

Fresh nutmeg, grated, for garnish

HOP-INFUSED GOSLING'S DARK RUM

+ Place the hops in a quart canning jar. Fill the jar with the rum and seal it shut.

+ After 1 hour, strain the mixture through a chinois into a fresh quart jar. Due to the alcohol content, this infusion should last indefinitely at room temperature.

YIELDS *About 750 ml*

1 ounce hops

750ml bottle Gosling's Dark Rum

BRANDY DAISY
À LA JOHNSON

Inspiration: Harry Johnson, *Bartenders' Manual*, 1882

Did someone order a Brandy Daisy, hold the ginger? In the world of Mr. Harry Johnson, the daisy walks hand in hand with Chartreuse, that mystical vegetal liqueur that began life in 1737 in a French monastic order but now finds more sociable adherents among craft cocktail bartenders. All Johnson's daisy recipes feature it, so we'll take his lead here.

In its green, 110 proof form, Chartreuse gives its name to the color chartreuse, not the other way around. Like Johnson, we're using the sweeter, 80 proof formulation, which is yellow, to keep closer to the daisy's requirements. Chartreuse is said to be composed of 130 herbs, flowers, and other plants, its recipe known only to the monks who still oversee its preparation today. Are sarsaparilla, dandelion, burdock, and lavender among those plants included? Let's not take any chances.

❊DIRECTIONS❊

✦ Add all the ingredients, except the soda and garnish, to a shaker. Fill with ice and shake. Add the soda to the shaker and strain the mixture into a punch glass with one chunk of cracked ice. Garnish with freshly grated nutmeg.

❊INGREDIENTS❊

1 dash Terra Firma Sarsaparilla Tincture

2 dashes Dr. Adam Elmegirab's Dandelion and Burdock Bitters

¾ ounce fresh lemon juice

1 ounce Yellow Chartreuse

1½ ounces Louis Royer VSOP Cognac

1½ ounces lavender soda

Fresh nutmeg, grated, for garnish

WHISKEY DAISY À LA FOUQUET

Inspiration: Louis Fouquet, *Bariana*, 1896

Rhubarb and raspberry have certain affinities, and here is our chance to augment the daisy structure to showcase them, modulated by orange as a second citrus. Fouquet's original resembles the Ward Eight cocktail, but our tug in the rhubarb direction changes that. This drink includes both a rhubarb root tincture and the commercial liqueur Rabarbaro Zucca, a lovely rhubarb-based amaro from Milan.

Fouquet specified Scotch, and in his annotations to the English edition, Charles Vexenat noted it was "surprising" that "raspberry and Scotch do not conflict." With rhubarb the conflict may rise again, so it's time to use the spicier yet harmonious rye instead.

DIRECTIONS

✦ Add all the ingredients, except the soda and garnish, to a shaker. Fill with ice and shake. Add the soda to the shaker and strain the mixture into a punch glass with one chunk of cracked ice. Garnish with freshly grated nutmeg.

INGREDIENTS

1 dash Rhubarb Root Tincture (see recipe at right)

2 dashes Bittermens Burlesque Bitters

½ ounce Raspberry Cordial (see page 66)

¾ ounce orange juice

1 ounce fresh lemon juice

½ ounce Rabarbaro Zucca

2½ ounces Wild Turkey Rye

1 ounce rhubarb soda

Fresh nutmeg, grated, for garnish

RHUBARB ROOT TINCTURE

✦ Combine the rhubarb root and Everclear in a jar. Allow to macerate for 3 days, then strain through a chinois into a fresh container. Add the water. Due to the alcohol content, this tincture should last indefinitely at room temperature.

YIELDS *About 10 ounces*

1 ounce powdered rhubarb root

4½ ounces Everclear

4½ ounces water

WHISKEY FIX
À LA STUART

Inspiration: Thomas Stuart, *Stuart's Fancy Drinks and How to Mix Them*, 1896

Since the distinguishing feature of a fix is its reliance on pineapple, that flavor must come through. Everything else is up for grabs, and here Jack has orchestrated six other ingredients all in the service of promoting, contrasting, and expanding on that pineapple basis.

Actually, there's only one fix in this chapter of "Fixes and Daisies," but it's a doozy. This time we're not afraid of using Scotch—we suggest a blend with a strong stance, such as the Great King Street brand—and we're backing it up with aquavit and sherry, too.

Scotch is often a difficult ingredient to mix with due to its own strong character. That's why Scotch cocktails are so few. And why a new one is so needed. Enjoy.

·❈DIRECTIONS❈·

⁕ Add all the ingredients, except the garnish, to a shaker. Fill with ice and shake. Strain into a punch glass with one chunk of cracked ice. Garnish with freshly grated nutmeg.

·❈INGREDIENTS❈·

¾ ounce Pineapple Cordial (see page 138)

3 dashes Chamomile Tincture (see page 80)

½ ounce fresh lemon juice

¾ ounce Aalborg Aquavit

¾ ounce Barbadillo Fino Sherry

1½ ounces Great King Street Blended Scotch

Fresh nutmeg, grated, for garnish

PINEAPPLE CORDIAL

+ Feed the pineapple chunks into an automatic juicer. Strain the juice through a chinois to remove pulp.

+ Add the pineapple juice, sugar, and water to a medium saucepan over medium heat, but do not boil. Slowly stir until the sugar has dissolved.

+ Remove from the heat. Use a funnel to pour into bottles. Add the Everclear and shake to mix. The cordial will keep for 2 to 3 weeks in the refrigerator.

YIELDS *About 26 ounces*

16 ounces pineapple chunks

2 cups granulated sugar

8 ounces water

½ ounce Everclear

SCOTCH DAISY

Inspiration: Thomas Stuart, *Stuart's Fancy Drinks and How to Mix Them*, 1896

Fruit syrups have been a valuable cornerstone to the mixed drink throughout its history. The daisy, indeed, was built well upon them. However, in this chapter, we've tried to show how an alternative to cloying syrup could be dry, sophisticated sherry, and the daisy could be built anew.

But okay, let's have of a bit of cloying syrup. Almond-flavored orgeat will do, complementing the nuttiness of the oloroso. There are many whiskey daisies in history to choose from, but Thomas Stuart's started with orgeat, and so shall we. There's also something appealing about combining the slightly tannic character of sherry with that of tea—altogether a mouth-watering contrivance.

DIRECTIONS

+ Add all the ingredients, except the soda and garnish, to a shaker. Fill with ice and shake. Add the soda to the shaker and strain the mixture into a punch glass with one chunk of cracked ice. Garnish with freshly grated nutmeg.

INGREDIENTS

2 ounces Masala Chai Tea–Infused Monkey Shoulder Scotch (see page 140)

¾ ounce Orgeat Syrup (see page 141)

1 ounce oloroso sherry

¾ ounce fresh lemon juice

3 dashes Dead Rabbit Orinoco Bitters or Angostura Aromatic Bitters

1 ounce vanilla bean soda

Fresh nutmeg, grated, for garnish

MASALA CHAI TEA–INFUSED MONKEY SHOULDER SCOTCH

* Place the tea bag in a quart canning jar. Fill the jar with Scotch and seal it shut.

* After 1 hour, remove the tea bag. Due to the alcohol content, this infusion should last indefinitely at room temperature.

YIELDS *About 750ml*

1 bag masala chai tea

750ml bottle Monkey Shoulder Scotch

ORGEAT SYRUP

+ Place the almonds in a large mixing bowl and cover with 4 cups of the hot water. Allow to sit for 30 minutes, then strain off the water.

+ Purée the almonds in a blender until smooth, adding the other 4 cups of hot water. Pour the water and almond mixture back into the mixing bowl and allow to sit for 2 hours.

+ Strain off the resulting "almond milk" using a chinois into a medium saucepan. You can discard the nut solids. Or put them into muffins.

+ Add the sugar to the saucepan over medium heat, but do not boil. Slowly stir until the sugar has dissolved.

+ When the syrup has thickened, remove from the heat. Strain through a chinois into bottles. Add the Everclear and orange flower water. The syrup will keep for 2 to 3 weeks in the refrigerator.

YIELDS _About 32 ounces_

8 ounces raw almonds, peeled and blanched

8 cups hot water

4 cups granulated sugar

½ ounce Everclear

Dash orange flower water

GIN DAISY
À LA PAUL

Inspiration: Charlie Paul, *Recipes of American and Other Iced Drinks*, 1902

At the time of the original 1902 recipe, genever was referred to in America as "Holland gin," so our lawyers advise me that this can be a Gin Daisy even without "gin" in it. (Of course, genever is gin's ancestor.) Originally an unpalatable malt wine, with juniper berries masking the taste, today's genevers show balance and nuance all the way through.

Gin's famous juniper infusion is still here, but genever packs additional muscle with its malt. Running further with that idea is the caraway-flavored kümmel and anise-flavored absinthe. Then the counterpoint to cut through this pungent, bready fog is the sharp snap of apricot eau de vie. Oh, if Charlie Paul could see us now.

DIRECTIONS

✦ Add all the ingredients, except the soda and garnish, to a shaker. Fill with ice and shake. Add the soda to the shaker and strain the mixture into a punch glass with one chunk of cracked ice. Garnish with freshly grated nutmeg.

INGREDIENTS

½ ounce Pistachio Syrup (see page 93)

3 dashes Pernod Absinthe

¾ ounce fresh lemon juice

½ ounce Combier Kümmel

¾ ounce Blume Marillen Apricot Eau de Vie

1½ ounces Bols Barrel-Aged Genever

1 ounce cucumber soda

Fresh nutmeg, grated, for garnish

LIVENER

Inspiration: Charlie Paul, *Recipes of American and Other Iced Drinks*, 1902

This drink fits the general profile of a daisy but with an entirely welcome innovation: Champagne. There are few beverages that Champagne cannot elevate, except perhaps Ovaltine, and Paul rightfully reaches for it in his original Livener recipe. To break the daisy monopoly on raspberry, let's try strawberry and rose instead, and finish with the inimitable stylings of Bittermens Burlesque Bitters, combining hibiscus, sour berries, and a hint of pepper. If you are not livened by this drink, you probably have already given up on life. Try another sip just to be sure.

DIRECTIONS

* Chill a Champagne flute in your freezer.

* Add all the ingredients, except the Champagne, to a shaker. Fill with ice and shake. Strain into the pre-chilled flute. Add the Champagne.

INGREDIENTS

1 ounce Strawberry Cordial (see page 89)

1½ ounces Rémy Martin VSOP Cognac

¼ ounce Combier Liqueur de Rose

¼ ounce Pernod Absinthe

¾ ounce fresh lemon juice

2 dashes Bittermens Burlesque Bitters

1½ ounces brut Champagne

EVENING DAISY

Inspiration: Tim Daly, *Daly's Bartenders' Encyclopedia*, 1903

There's no need to wait for sundown to mix up the first Evening Daisy of the day. In fact, refreshing as it is, you may find a need for it much, much earlier.

True to the formula Jack has employed in this group of drinks, the dichotomy is set up between the herbal and the juicy, with woodsy nettles, fennel, and absinthe rubbing shoulders with lemon, cucumber, and elderflower. Our friends at Bittermens contribute the Boston Bittahs, a citrus and chamomile concoction which effortlessly slides into both sides of the flavor mix. Of course, the stalwart heart of it all is Jameson Black Barrel Whiskey, an Irish powerhouse that has spent time in charred oak barrels like its American bourbon cousins.

DIRECTIONS

+ Add all the ingredients, except the soda water and garnish, to a shaker. Fill with ice and shake. Add the soda water to the shaker and strain the mixture into a punch glass with one chunk of cracked ice. Garnish with freshly grated nutmeg.

INGREDIENTS

2 ounces Nettle Tea–Infused Jameson Black Barrel Whiskey (see recipe at right)

½ ounce Fennel Syrup (see recipe at right)

½ ounce Cucumber Juice (see page 148)

½ ounce elderflower liqueur

¼ ounce Pernod Absinthe

1 ounce fresh lemon juice

3 dashes Bittermens Boston Bittahs

1½ ounces soda water

Fresh nutmeg, grated, for garnish

NETTLE TEA–INFUSED JAMESON BLACK BARREL WHISKEY

* Place the tea bag in a quart canning jar. Fill the jar with the whiskey and seal it shut.

* After 1 hour, remove the tea bag. Due to the alcohol content, this infusion should last indefinitely at room temperature.

YIELDS *About 750ml*

1 bag nettle tea

750ml bottle Jameson Black Barrel Whiskey

FENNEL SYRUP

* Add all the ingredients to a medium saucepan over medium heat, but do not boil. Slowly stir until the sugar has dissolved.

* Remove the pan from the heat, cover, and let the fennel seeds steep for 15 minutes. Strain through a chinois into bottles. The syrup will keep for 2 to 3 weeks in the refrigerator.

YIELDS *About 16 ounces*

2 cups water

2 cups granulated sugar

½ ounce fennel seeds

CUCUMBER JUICE

• Peel the cucumbers with a vegetable peeler. It's important to remove all of the skin as it has a different flavor from the inside.

• Slice off both ends of the cucumbers and discard them. Chop the cucumbers into 1-inch chunks. (When in doubt, smaller is better.)

• Blend the chunks in a food processor or blender on medium speed for about 2 minutes, or until you have a pulpy liquid.

• Using your chinois, strain the pulp into a large bowl. Use a spoon to stir the pulp, as well as to press all the liquid from it.

• Bottle and store in the refrigerator for up to 1 week.

YIELDS *About 16 ounces*

3 medium cucumbers

BYRRH WINE DAISY

Inspiration: J. A. Grohusko, *Jack's Manual of Recipes for Fancy Mixed Drinks and How to Serve Them*, 1908

Here is a grand testament to the value of the apéritif in mixed drinks—even though we present the recipe as the final "digestif" in this chapter. In this drink we will combine two famous liqueurs, the French Byrrh of the title (pronounced, somewhat disappointingly, like *beer*) and the Italian amaro, Ciociaro. Byrrh is a fortified red wine with a light dose of quinine, making it a kind of bottled claret and tonic. Among all its herbal constituents, Amaro Ciociaro smacks principally of bitter orange and cinnamon, though its recipe is of course a trade secret. With that battle of the titans already unfolding, we have stepped back the traditional raspberry syrup to a drier eau de vie.

To keep up with those professionally hewn herbal liqueurs, a less common botanical is specified here. *Angelica archangelica* grows sweetly scented roots that have made it a favorite of herbalists through the ages, especially before the widespread availability of sugar as a sweetener.

John Parkinson, a founding member of the Worshipful Society of Apothecaries, wrote a 1629 botanical tract notable for two endowments: the completeness with which he cataloged all plants known to flourish in England, and the horrifying Latin pun in its title, *Paradisi in Sole Paradisus Terrestris*—literally, "Park-in-Sun's Terrestrial Paradise." Nonetheless, in that volume he put angelica before all other herbs for its medicinal benefit to just about any complaint. Now, almost 400 years later, angelica root will be famous again when you ask for it at your local health food store.

The daisy is a flexible category that in these pages has supported everything from sherry to amari. We hope you have enjoyed following this daisy chain.

DIRECTIONS

+ Add all the ingredients, except the soda and garnish, to a shaker. Fill with ice and shake. Add the soda to the shaker and strain the mixture into a punch glass with one chunk of cracked ice. Garnish with freshly grated nutmeg.

INGREDIENTS

3 dashes Angelica Tincture (see recipe below)

¾ ounce orange juice

¾ ounce fresh lemon juice

1 ounce F. Meyer Framboise Eau de Vie

1 ounce Amaro Ciociaro

1 ounce Byrrh Grand Quinquina

1 ounce rhubarb soda

Fresh nutmeg, grated, for garnish

ANGELICA TINCTURE

+ Combine the angelica root and Everclear in a jar. Allow to macerate for 3 days, then strain through a chinois into a fresh container. Add the water. Due to the alcohol content, this tincture should last indefinitely at room temperature.

YIELDS *About 10 ounces*

1 ounce powdered angelica root

4½ ounces Everclear

4½ ounces water

CUPS AND COBBLERS

Having dispatched the drinks descended from punch, let's jump back in time to analyze other formulations that competed with punch for the gullets of the worthy. Cups and cobblers go together because they feature beer and wine. In the contemporary era those may not be common ingredients in mixed drinks, but in days of yore they were essential. The sugared cobbler was first made with wine and fortified wine, especially sherry. Cups, an even older form, could feature wine, beer, or both. Cups have their origins in social drinking—toasting at formal gatherings. Cobblers are just as delicious on your own.

Cups and cobblers are our opportunity to resurrect not just a category, but a different style of drinking, and (regardless of the number of ingredients) a refreshing, lower alcohol one at that. Offering more a kiss than a kick, these drinks might be considered for duty as what cocktailian *capo* Gary Regan terms "session beverages"—something you can stick with all night.

However, in this section, we've merged the best elements of each. The original cobblers were simple conglomerations of ice, sugar, and spirit, decorated with fresh fruit. As you should know, we love the simple but we saw our own approach to mixed drinks as expansive. So while there will be plenty of fruit decoration in the historical cobbler vein in the next pages, the drinks' format is in keeping with our Rococo maximalist style.

Such a property is ascribed to cups in William Terrington's seminal *Cooling Cups and Dainty Drinks*, as he notes their role in "the convivial usages of the ancients"—they "took three cups at their banquets: one, to allay thirst; another, for pleasure; and a third, as a libation to Jupiter Servator." All the following drinks are appropriate for this tripartite use.

For more exploration of wine in mixed drinks, see the chapter on bishops.

TWEEN DECK

Inspiration: William Terrington, *Cooling Cups and Dainty Drinks*, 1869

We begin with a selection from Terrington, the acknowledged commander of the cup.

This drink has a maritime moniker, so be prepared for your daily ration of rum. This is a bit like an antique rum punch: spicy, citrusy, and not afraid of gales rippling the rigging.

Once again, we're using three rums to approximate the style of Jamaican rum that would have been known at the time—itself much closer to a robust, funky naval spec than the sweet, clean rums favored by most today.

This is a hearty brew for stout fellows, and we recommend stowing a ration or two in your hold as you prepare to run up three sheets in heavy weather.

DIRECTIONS

‣ Add all the ingredients, except the garnishes, to a mixing glass. Fill with ice and stir until chilled. Strain into an ice-filled tall glass. Garnish with citrus slices, seasonal berries, pineapple chunks, grapes, and freshly grated nutmeg.

INGREDIENTS

¾ ounce Lime Sherbet (see page 109)

3 dashes Allspice Tincture (see page 123)

3 dashes Dead Rabbit Orinoco Bitters or Angostura Aromatic Bitters

¼ ounce fresh lime juice

½ ounce Smith & Cross Jamaican Rum

½ ounce Banks 7 Rum

½ ounce Cruzan Blackstrap Rum

3 ounces cask ale

Citrus slices, seasonal berries, pineapple chunks, and grapes, for garnish

Fresh nutmeg, grated, for garnish

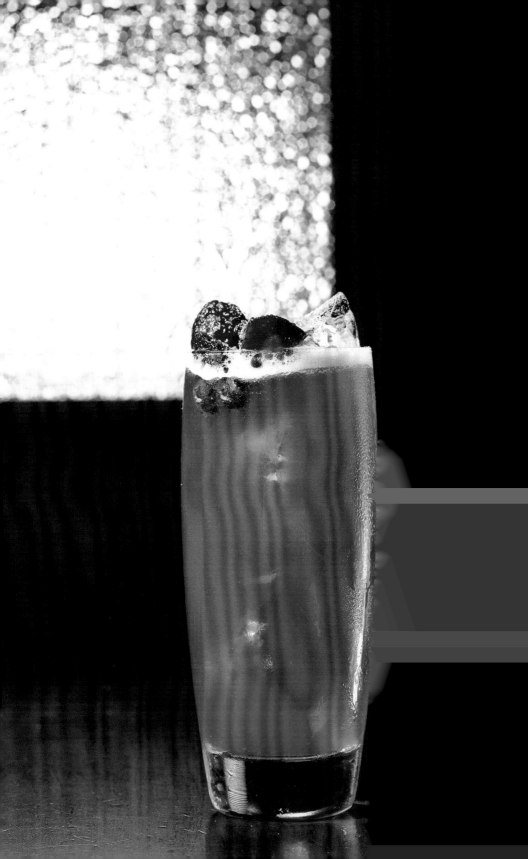

MOSELLE
À LA PORTER

Inspiration: Henry Porter and George Edwin Roberts, *Cups and Their Customs*, 1863

Messrs. Porter and Roberts are men that we can understand. They undertook their study, *Cups and Their Customs*, not just to record and analyze pleasant drinks that they enjoyed, nor even to chronicle the best habits of their era for posterity. Their aim, they state in their introduction, is no less than to replace "that stereotyped drinking which at present holds sway at the festive boards of England." We, too, hate the notion of stereotyped drinking when there is so much else in the annals of, as Porter and Roberts name it, "Bacchanology." Let us have iconoclastic drinking, and let us start with this delicious cup.

Their Moselle cup is a kind of sangría, with orange, black currant, and herbs left to steep in a bottle of wine. The herbs originally used were mint, sage, and borage (an herb delicately reminiscent of cucumber). We've adapted this as we often do, using a combination of sherbet, tincture, tea, and liqueur to deliver those same gently crisp flavors with a richer variety of textures.

The original recipe calls for wine from a production region along the Moselle River in France, a Rhine tributary that also borders wine-producing territory in Luxembourg and Germany. We've updated this with the bone-dry Mosel Sekt, Germany's sparkling version, to counterbalance the range of sweet fruit.

⁂ DIRECTIONS ⁂

✦ Add all the ingredients, except the sekt and garnishes, to a mixing glass. Fill with ice and stir until chilled. Add the sekt to the mixing glass and strain the mixture into an ice-filled wine glass. Garnish with citrus slices, seasonal berries, pineapple chunks, grapes, and freshly grated nutmeg.

⁂ INGREDIENTS ⁂

½ ounce Orange Sherbet (see recipe at right)

3 dashes Sage Tincture (see recipe at right)

¾ ounce fresh lemon juice

¾ ounce peppermint tea, cold

¼ ounce Combier Crème de Cassis

3 ounces Mosel Sekt

Citrus slices, seasonal berries, pineapple chunks, and grapes, for garnish

Fresh nutmeg, grated, for garnish

ORANGE SHERBET

✦ Prepare an oleo-saccharum with the orange peels and sugar (see page 64). In a small saucepan, combine the oleo-saccharum and orange juice over medium heat, but do not boil. Slowly stir to dissolve the sugar. Remove from the heat when the sugar has fully dissolved. Strain through a chinois into bottles. The sherbet will keep for 2 to 3 weeks in the refrigerator.

2 oranges
1 cup granulated sugar
8 ounces orange juice

YIELDS *About 20 ounces*

SAGE TINCTURE

✦ Combine the sage and Everclear in a jar. Allow to macerate for 3 days, then strain through a chinois into a fresh container. Add the water. Due to the alcohol content, this tincture should last indefinitely at room temperature.

1 ounce powered sage
4½ ounces Everclear
4½ ounces water

YIELDS *About 10 ounces*

RED CUP

Inspiration: Richard Cook, *Oxford Night Caps*, 1835

Oxford Night Caps was reprinted almost continuously between 1827 and 1931, and no doubt more repeatedly turned to than most undergraduate texts. In the book, Richard Cook outlines not just drinking as it was done in Oxford in his era, but further back in the generations, as many of those drinks were already old traditions by his day.

Cook indicates that refreshing cups were needed by Oxford University students who undertook excursions along the Thames, in so doing passing many a waterfront pub. He informs us, "Many are the sonnets and songs which have been made upon the fair waiting women who almost invariably prepare this cooling and wholesome beverage." This just shows how the art of chatting up the server has fallen down in the last couple of centuries. However, the verse Cook quotes has nothing on the scribe's work on behalf of Susie Drake (see "Florodora," page 120), suggesting that ordering a drink sometimes can be more heroic even than serving it:

> She looks up the oars, and the old tavern scores,
> And now and then cleans out a wherry [a small river boat];
> > The sails she can mend,
> > And the parlour attend,
> For obliging's the Maid of the Ferry.
> She serves at the bar, and excels all by far
> In making Cold Tankard of perry [pear cider];
> > How sweet then at eve,
> > With her leave to receive
> A kiss from the Maid of the Ferry.

The Cold Tankard was a drink combining hard apple or pear cider with lemon juice, sugar, and brandy. Like the original Moselle cup, it also featured borage, which was so important in flavoring the cups of the era that a sprig of it was depicted on the frontispiece to *Cups and Their Customs*.

For the Red Cup, the tavern maid would substitute port wine and redcurrant jelly for the cider in the Cold Tankard. We've taken her cue and are using cucumber juice and soda instead of borage, and Calvados instead of brandy. Calvados brings back the all-important orchard scent we lost with the replacement of cider and perry.

DIRECTIONS

+ Add all the ingredients, except the soda and garnishes, to a shaker. Fill with ice and shake. Add the soda to the shaker and strain the mixture into an ice-filled tall glass. Garnish with citrus slices, seasonal berries, pineapple chunks, grapes, and freshly grated nutmeg.

INGREDIENTS

¾ ounce Cucumber Juice (see page 148)

½ ounce Lemon Sherbet (see page 71)

1 teaspoon redcurrant jelly

¾ ounce fresh lemon juice

¾ ounce Graham's Late Bottled Vintage Port

1½ ounces Château du Breuil VSOP Calvados

1½ ounces cucumber soda

Citrus slices, seasonal berries, pineapple chunks, and grapes, for garnish

Fresh nutmeg, grated, for garnish

RED CUP NO. 2

Inspiration: William Terrington, *Cooling Cups and Dainty Drinks*, 1869

As an example of the constant creative reinvention of drink concepts that characterizes the work of Muldoon and McGarry, here's a different take on the same general combination of flavors as the previous recipe. Like the Cold Tankard that inspired the Red Cup in 1835, this Red Cup No. 2 gathers together red berries, tartness (in the form of lemon and elderflower), and aromas of the grove (here, quince and pear).

Then it dumps a depth charge of Jameson Black Barrel Whiskey into it. Ladies and gentlemen, you are not boating along the Thames, this is Dead Rabbit country. Please keep your personal belongings with you at all times.

❈ DIRECTIONS ❈

+ Add all the ingredients, except for the Cidre Poire and garnishes, to a shaker. Fill with ice and shake. Add the Cidre Poire to the shaker and strain the mixture into an ice-filled wine glass. Garnish with seasonal berries and freshly grated nutmeg.

❈ INGREDIENTS ❈

1½ ounces Hibiscus-Infused Jameson Black Barrel Whiskey (see page 163)

¼ ounce Lemon Sherbet (see page 71)

¾ ounce cranberry liqueur

¼ ounce elderflower liqueur

¾ ounce fresh lemon juice

1 teaspoon quince jelly

3 dashes Bittermens Burlesque Bitters

1½ ounces Christian Drouin Cidre Poire

Seasonal berries, for garnish

Fresh nutmeg, grated, for garnish

HIBISCUS-INFUSED JAMESON BLACK BARREL WHISKEY

+ Place the tea bag in a quart canning jar. Fill the jar with the whiskey and seal it shut.

+ After 1 hour, remove the tea bag. Due to the alcohol content, this infusion should last indefinitely at room temperature.

YIELDS *About 750ml*

1 bag hibiscus tea

750ml bottle Jameson Black Barrel Whiskey

CIDER NO. 4

Inspiration: William Terrington, *Cooling Cups and Dainty Drinks*, 1869

If the previous cups were red, then this one is green. As in the Red Cup No. 2, the juggling of similar ingredients but with different emphasis has created a totally new experience. This is a light, crisp sip of summer.

Keep in mind that in America, "cider" generally means unfiltered, unclarified apple juice with no alcohol content. This has been the case since Prohibition, previous to which our definition fit the rest of the English-speaking world's: Cider was booze, a fermented beverage made from apples just as wine is made from grapes. Another word unfamiliar to our ears is "perry," signifying cider made from pears. Now making a bit of a comeback stateside as "hard cider," these ingredients were crucial for cups of the nineteenth century on both sides of the Atlantic.

One of our favorite brands is Christian Drouin Cidre Poire, pressed in Normandy from three pear varietals and left unfiltered.

DIRECTIONS

+ Add all the ingredients, except the Cidre Poire and garnishes, to a shaker. Fill with ice and shake. Add the Cidre Poire to the shaker and strain the mixture into an ice-filled wine glass. Garnish with citrus slices, seasonal berries, pineapple chunks, grapes, and freshly grated nutmeg.

INGREDIENTS

½ ounce Lemon Sherbet (see page 71)

¾ ounce Cucumber Juice (see page 148)

1 teaspoon quince jelly

½ ounce lemon juice

1½ ounces F. Meyer Poire Williams Eau de Vie

1½ ounces Christian Drouin Cidre Poire

Citrus slices, seasonal berries, pineapple chunks, and grapes, for garnish

Fresh nutmeg, grated, for garnish

CLARET CUP
À LA FOUQUET

Inspiration: Louis Fouquet, *Bariana*, 1896

Stepping from the orchard to the vineyard, let's consider the class of drink known as the Claret Cup. It's included in both *Cups and Their Customs* and *Oxford Night Caps*. Terrington's *Cooling Cups and Dainty Drinks* even lists twenty variations for different occasions. The basic recipe (red wine, lemon, sugar, and soda water) invites experimentation with all manner of liqueurs, spices, herbs, and other spirits—and, of course, borage.

Even after all the offerings of that English consortium of Terrington, Porter, Roberts, and Cook, we found it was a Frenchman's recipe we identified with most. Simple and delicious.

Louis Fouquet made his "Louis' Claret Cup" with kirsch, a dry cherry brandy. We've agreed with this approach, but our dry is a tart raspberry eau de vie in concert with a sweeter cherry liqueur for a more complex fruit flavor on the secure base of sturdy Bordeaux.

DIRECTIONS

✦ Add all the ingredients, except the garnishes, to a shaker. Fill with ice and shake. Strain into an ice-filled tall glass. Garnish with seasonal berries and freshly grated nutmeg. Serve with a straw.

INGREDIENTS

¾ ounce Lemon Sherbet (see page 71)

½ ounce fresh lemon juice

¼ ounce Roi Rene Cherry Liqueur

½ ounce F. Meyer Framboise Eau de Vie

2 ounces Red Bordeaux

Seasonal berries, for garnish

Fresh nutmeg, grated, for garnish

SAUTERNE À LA RICKET

Inspiration: E. Ricket and C. Thomas, *The Gentleman's Table Guide*, 1871

"Sauterne" is an intentionally misspelled American generic term for white wine, meant to evoke (but apparently outside the bounds of fraud) the famous Sauternes dessert wines from the Sauternais region of Bordeaux. We'll stay ecumenical and instead suggest the non-sauterne, non-Sauternes fortified dessert wine, Muscat de Beaumes-de-Venise.

In the vision of Ricket and Thomas, this wine cup was introduced to tangerines, Benedictine, soda water, and, of course, borage—although woodruff could be considered instead. We considered it at once.

Woodruff, *Galium odoratum*, is known for its sweet fragrance that resembles freshly mown hay. In Germany, it is used to flavor everything from wine and beer to ice cream to sausages. We will settle for five dashes of its tincture.

But you just can't say goodbye to borage. Cucumber soda will do here in its remembrance.

Tradition and innovation have combined in this sweetly refreshing drink.

❈ DIRECTIONS ❈

✦ Add all the ingredients, except the soda and garnishes, to a shaker. Fill with ice and shake. Add the soda to the shaker and strain the mixture into an ice-filled tall glass. Garnish with citrus slices, seasonal berries, pineapple chunks, grapes, and freshly grated nutmeg.

❈ INGREDIENTS ❈

½ ounce Tangerine Sherbet (see page 169)

5 dashes Woodruff Tincture (see page 169)

½ ounce clementine juice

¾ ounce fresh lemon juice

¼ ounce Benedictine DOM

2½ ounces Muscat de Beaumes-de-Venise

1½ ounces cucumber soda

Citrus slices, seasonal berries, pineapple chunks, and grapes, for garnish

Fresh nutmeg, grated, for garnish

TANGERINE SHERBET

+ Prepare an oleo-saccharum with the tangerine peels and sugar (see page 64).

+ In a small saucepan, combine the oleo-saccharum and tangerine juice over medium heat, but do not boil. Slowly stir to dissolve the sugar. Remove from the heat when the sugar has fully dissolved. Strain through a chinois into bottles. The sherbet will keep for 2 to 3 weeks in the refrigerator.

4 tangerines
1¼ cups granulated sugar
10 ounces tangerine juice

YIELDS *About 20 ounces*

WOODRUFF TINCTURE

+ Combine the woodruff and Everclear in a jar. Allow to macerate for 3 days, then strain through a chinois into a fresh container. Add the water. Due to the alcohol content, this tincture should last indefinitely at room temperature.

1 ounce dried woodruff
4½ ounces Everclear
4½ ounces water

YIELDS *About 10 ounces*

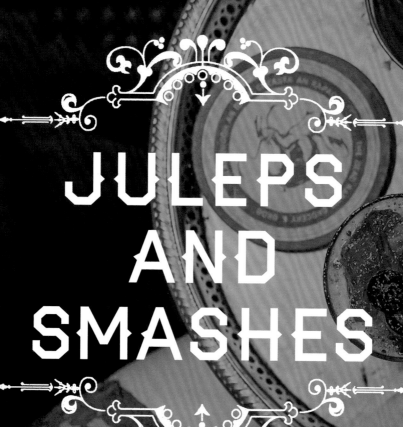

JULEPS
AND
SMASHES

Whether it's a smash or a julep, one thing's certain: Some mint is getting smacked.

The word "julep" entered English from the Persian word for rose water, *gulab*, and for most of history always referred to medicinal drafts. The modern sense of an alcoholic beverage no doubt came along in the usual comedic way of comparing boozing to a cure; e.g., "take two of these and call me in the morning." The Mint Julep, an American invention still zealously celebrated today, started life as a brandy or rum drink and was only much later converted to the whiskey for which it's known down Kentucky way.

The basic format for both categories is spirit, sugar, and mint. The smash can be thought of as a short julep; it's a gulp and go, not a sipper. Unlike a julep, it wouldn't have time to trouble with a straw.

These are our mint drinks. Both categories were high fashion for much of the nineteenth century, making them a must for our list—and you'll see (and taste) why.

JULEP À LA THOMAS

Inspiration: Jerry Thomas, *The Bar Tenders' Guide*, 1862

The Mint Julep flourished in the middle of the nineteenth century, so we must turn to that bartender who also had his glory days at that time. Professor Thomas shows us the way with his original julep, one of the few categories of drink to get an introductory discussion in his book (noble punch being another). Thomas points out the importance of the drink to the American South, a sentiment which is echoed evermore when the julep is mentioned.

Sentimentalization of the Mint Julep in the South seems to be constant even as the centuries pass. Perhaps this has something to do with its connection to a pastoral "good old days," as exemplified in the famous description of the Mint Julep from a letter by General Simon Bolivar Buckner on March 30, 1937, in which he lays out the druidic quest for ingredients from nature's Southland bounty:

"Go to a spring where cool, crystal-clear water bubbles from under a bank of dew-washed ferns. In a consecrated vessel, dip up a little water at the source. Follow the stream thru its banks of green moss and wild flowers until it broadens and trickles thru beds of mint growing in an aromatic profusion and waving softly in the summer breeze. Gather the sweetest and tenderest shoots."

Of course, the spearmint typically used in drinks is a European and Asian species not native to North America, and neither sugar syrup nor bourbon can be gathered wild, which leaves the only ingredient that is both indigenous and wild to be water. Nonetheless, the "agrarian dream" of the julep survives.

Irvin S. Cobb, a kind of humorist of his day, goes further in *Irvin S. Cobb's Own Recipe Book* of 1934, theorizing that "the Civil War was not brought on by Secession or Slavery or the State's Rights issue. . . . It was brought on by some Yankee coming down South and putting nutmeg in a julep." As strong believers in the primacy of both human equality and nutmeg, we are not amused by Irvin S. Cobb.

There are many controversies over the preparation of a proper julep; the type of spirit is the least of them. One we are prepared to wade into is whether the mint should be manhandled privately or only as part of the general drink-making. In other words, do you crush or bruise the mint ahead of time, to bring out the oils? Or will this happen anyway while it is being banged around with ice in a shaker?

Thomas is a bruiser; in this recipe we suggest skipping that step and loading your mint into the shaker to be bruised in due course.

Thomas also specified his Mint Julep with brandy (which is, of course, delicious in its own way). We will bow to Big Bourbon because its woody flavor works wonderfully with the contrasting addition of absinthe and Parfait Amour. This is a Mint Julep like no one in a big hat near some horses has experienced.

❈DIRECTIONS❈

✦ Add all the ingredients, except the garnishes, to a shaker. Fill with ice and shake. Strain into a tall glass filled with crushed ice. Garnish with citrus slices, seasonal berries, and mint springs. Dust with powdered sugar and serve with a straw.

❈INGREDIENTS❈

½ ounce Eau de Thé Syrup (see page 80)

4 fresh mint leaves

3 dashes Pernod Absinthe

¼ ounce Parfait Amour

2½ ounces Buffalo Trace Bourbon

Citrus slices, seasonal berries, and fresh mint sprigs, for garnish

Powdered sugar, for garnish

CRITERION À LA FOUQUET

Inspiration: Louis Fouquet, *Bariana*, 1896

The Criterion was the Paris bar where Louis Fouquet held court in the 1890s, and this is his Rum Smash recipe. (Interestingly, the Criterion was also the name of the London bar where Leo Engel held sway. We are proud to base drinks on these masterful Criteria. Both are still around today, although Paris' is now named after its famous barman.)

A Rum Smash is essentially a short Mojito with notable renovations. We're dialing up the funk with an aged *rhum agricole*, so named because it is made from sugar cane itself rather than the molasses created as a result of sugar production. This different approach gives *rhum agricole* a pleasantly grassy note. It's a style of rum associated with the historically French Caribbean possessions and is therefore in keeping with the probable contents of M. Fouquet's bar shelves.

DIRECTIONS

+ Add all the ingredients, except the garnish, to a shaker. Fill with ice and shake. Strain into a punch glass. Garnish with freshly grated nutmeg.

INGREDIENTS

2 dashes Eucalyptus Tincture (see page 75)

¾ ounce Lime Sherbet (see page 109)

6 to 8 fresh mint leaves

½ ounce fresh lime juice

2½ ounces Rhum JM VSOP

Fresh nutmeg, grated, for garnish

PINEAPPLE À LA THOMAS

Inspiration: Jerry Thomas, *The Bar Tenders' Guide*, 1862

Thomas' Pineapple Julep is a strange concoction. It's not really a julep, for one thing, as it has no mint and is based on gin. The pineapple is mostly for décor. Aimed at five people instead of our individual serving, it seems more of a party centerpiece than something to get the party started.

Jack knew there was something here, but he wasn't sure what it was at first, so he stripped it right down to its core flavors and built it back up anew. Orange juice was replaced with orange bitters, raspberry cordial was replaced with raspberry eau de vie backed with rose water, and the pineapple flavor was reinforced with pineapple cordial. Mint was introduced, bringing us back to orthodox taxonomy. However, gin was still out—leaving the drink to rest on its eaux de vie and gentian liqueur as a new base.

All that makes Pineapple à la Thomas the most challengingly flavored drink in the chapter, with the bitter element of gentian contrasting against many layers of fruit and flower.

❖ DIRECTIONS ❖

+ Add all the ingredients, except the sekt, to a shaker. Fill with ice and shake. Add the sekt and strain the mixture into a punch glass.

❖ INGREDIENTS ❖

2 dashes Chamomile Tincture (see page 80)

½ ounce Pineapple Cordial (see page 138)

4 to 6 fresh mint leaves

2 dashes orange bitters

1 drop rose water

½ ounce F. Meyer Framboise Eau de Vie

½ ounce F. Meyer Kirsch Eau de Vie

¾ ounce Aveze Gentiane

2 ounces Mosel Sekt

WHISKEY SMASH À LA TERRINGTON

Inspiration: William Terrington, *Cooling Cups and Dainty Drinks*, 1869

Terrington's original recipe calls for a sprig of verbena in addition to mint. Many species are in the verbena genus, but he probably was referring to *Verbena officinalis*, revered since antiquity as a medicinal plant with relaxing properties. Yet tansy, a cheerful yellow button flower with a peppery taste, suits us better.

Jack's version is also influenced by the whiskey smashes made by Dale "King Cocktail" DeGroff in recent years. DeGroff used muddled mint as well as muddled lemons. To keep our recipe consistent with the general plan, lemon sherbet and juice replace the crushed fruit. This is also delicious and cuts down on incidents of muddler's elbow in the workplace.

✤ DIRECTIONS ✤

✦ Add all the ingredients, except the garnish, to a shaker. Fill with ice and shake. Strain into a punch glass. Garnish with freshly grated nutmeg.

✤ INGREDIENTS ✤

3 dashes Tansy Tincture (see recipe below)

¾ ounce Lemon Sherbet (see page 71)

6 to 8 fresh mint leaves

½ ounce fresh lemon juice

2½ ounces Bulleit Rye Whiskey

Fresh nutmeg, grated, for garnish

TANSY TINCTURE

✦ Combine the tansy and Everclear in a jar. Allow to macerate for 3 days, then strain through a chinois into a fresh container. Due to the alcohol content, this tincture should last indefinitely at room temperature.

1 ounce dried tansy

4½ ounces Everclear

4½ ounces water

YIELDS *About 10 ounces*

PINEAPPLE AND ROSEMARY SMASH

Inspiration: William Terrington, *Cooling Cups and Dainty Drinks*, 1869

Jack was inspired to create another combination of complex flavors after the success of his Pineapple à la Thomas. This drink is based on the principles of the smash as Terrington relates them, but not to any Terrington drink in particular. Here, the herbal forces, marshaled by Chartreuse and rosemary, battle the formidable fruit flavors of lemon and pineapple, refereed by good old mint. Of course, it is all a friendly contest and the true victor is the lifter of the glass.

❧DIRECTIONS❧

✦ Pre-chill a punch glass. Add all the ingredients, except the garnish, to a shaker. Fill with ice and shake. Strain into the punch glass. Garnish with freshly grated nutmeg.

❧INGREDIENTS❧

5 dashes Rosemary Tincture (see recipe below)

¾ ounce Lemon Sherbet (see page 71)

2 ounces Bols Genever

½ ounce Green Chartreuse

¾ ounce fresh lemon juice

¾ ounce pineapple juice

6 to 8 fresh mint leaves

Fresh nutmeg, grated, for garnish

ROSEMARY TINCTURE

✦ Combine the rosemary and Everclear in a jar. Allow to macerate for 3 days, then strain through a chinois into a fresh container. Add the water. Due to the alcohol content, this tincture should last indefinitely at room temperature.

1 ounce dried rosemary

4½ ounces Everclear

4½ ounces water

YIELDS *About 10 ounces*

GIN SMASH À LA BYRON

Inspiration: O. H. Byron, *The Modern Bartenders' Guide or Fancy Drinks and How to Mix Them*, 1884

Smashing right along, here's a fresh, vegetal take on the category. The Gin Smash is reminiscent of the modern Southside, but we've taken it in our own direction with genever and verdant notes.

Of course, in 1884, gin would have more likely than not been "Holland" style, or genever. After analyzing the structure of Byron's original, we realigned it in the same manner as the preceding Criterion (page 175) and Whiskey Smash (page 178). Some may say that these smashes are not strictly historically accurate, but as ever, our goal is to draw inspiration from the historical sources, rather than to simply repeat them. We think you will find our version bracing and in touch with whichever era you're drinking it in.

DIRECTIONS

* Add all the ingredients, except the garnish, to a shaker. Fill with ice and shake. Strain into a punch glass. Garnish with freshly grated nutmeg.

INGREDIENTS

¾ ounce Lemon Sherbet (see page 71)

3 dashes Bittermens Orchard Street Celery Shrub

6 to 8 fresh mint leaves

½ ounce fresh lemon juice

2½ ounce Bols Genever

Fresh nutmeg, grated, for garnish

CHAMPAGNE À LA FOUQUET

Inspiration: Louis Fouquet, *Bariana*, 1896

A challenging drink for Champagne lovers, this is based on a Brandy Julep but lengthened with the bubbly stuff. Our recipe combines three esteemed French contributions to the cocktail cornucopia: Cognac, Champagne, and Chartreuse.

Louis Fouquet liked Yellow Chartreuse in his juleps, and we follow his lead here, but the Champagne is Jack's own Gallic gifting. Eau de Thé syrup adds a distinct grassy note that works well with the Chartreuse, adding another dimension not seen in most traditional juleps.

We are far from the hills of Kentucky now, but that only shows how flexible the julep can be when unchained from sectional tradition. We've seen it brandied about, herbalized, and seconded to a pineapple, but our final preparation is to be raised in Champagne salute to the historic julep.

DIRECTIONS

+ Add all the ingredients, except the Champagne and garnishes, to a shaker. Shake vigorously. Add the Champagne and strain the mixture into a tall glass filled with crushed ice. Garnish with citrus slices, seasonal berries, and mint springs. Dust with powdered sugar and serve with a straw.

INGREDIENTS

¼ ounce Eau de Thé Syrup (see page 80)

4 to 6 fresh mint leaves

½ ounce Yellow Chartreuse

2 ounces Rémy Martin 1738 Cognac

2 ounces Piper Heidsieck Cuvée brut Champagne

Citrus slices, seasonal berries, and fresh mint sprigs, for garnish

Powdered sugar, for garnish

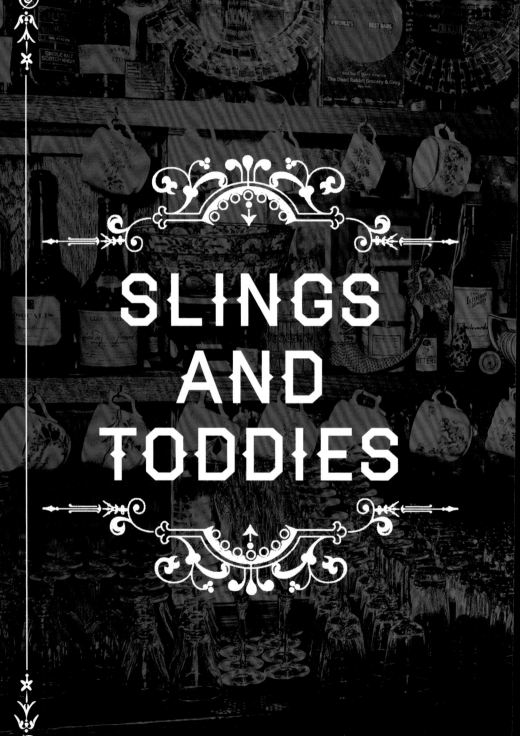

SLINGS AND TODDIES

These categories are united by their completely pared down set of ingredients: spirit, water, and sugar. That's as basic as one can imagine a mixed drink being and still meriting the name.

A chief distinction is that a toddy incorporates still water and a sling carbonated water. Additionally, the toddy eschews all lemon peels and generally ends up with nutmeg on top whereas the sling has the reverse. (Of course, in this book we have already shown that a mixed drink needs nutmeg only slightly less than it needs a container to be poured into.) Also, although today we think of a toddy as being hot, both drinks were served both hot and cold.

In the next pages, however, we have taken the advice of that tutor of the toddy and savant of the sling, David Wondrich, in calling the hot ones toddies and the cold one slings. In this way, the craft evolves.

HOT WHISKEY TODDY

Inspiration: Jerry Thomas, *The Bar-Tender's Guide*, 1862

You don't have to be crazy for cocktails to have heard of a Hot Toddy. It's been around for more than a couple of hundred years and there have been many cold nights since where it has played a role. And whiskey, at least in America which loved that stuff so, would be its default spirit.

However, Jerry Thomas describes four toddies and three slings in his famous guide, with some toddies being specified as hot but some as cold, and the same for the slings. Despite this variety, one drink he does *not* include is anything called a Hot Whiskey Toddy, though he has a Whiskey Toddy (cold) and a Hot Whiskey Sling—which oddly enough is the only of the three slings to be hot. So, let us cut through this tangled taxonomy of 1862 and create a drink that we all know ought to exist—hot whiskey.

A proper hot toddy needs a strongly flavored base, since it will be diluted with water. Islay Scotch is a common solution, with its rich, peaty flavor. Ireland offers its own peated, pot still spirits (see Punch à la Taylor on page 74 for a discussion), and here we've chosen the excellent Connemara with those attributes. We will also be dressing up the spartan structure of the historical toddy with McGarry touches of herb and fruit for a more nuanced experience. All these flavors will be wafted along in the hot steam, for an extraordinarily aromatic drink.

❈DIRECTIONS❈

+ Add all the ingredients, except the hot water and garnish, to a wine glass and stir. Add the hot water. Garnish with freshly grated nutmeg.

❈INGREDIENTS❈

2 dashes Mace Tincture (see page 77)

½ ounce Lemon Sherbet (see page 71)

1½ ounces Connemara Peated Single Malt Irish Whiskey

¼ ounce pear eau de vie

2 dashes Dead Rabbit Orinoco Bitters or Angostura Aromatic Bitters

3 ounces hot water

Fresh nutmeg, grated, for garnish

HOT BUTTERED BLACKSTRAP

Inspiration: Jerry Thomas, *The Bar-Tender's Guide*, 1862

This drink is the luxurious combination of a Hot Whiskey Toddy and a Hot Buttered Rum in one convenient glass. Who says we can't have it all in the fast-paced contemporary world?

✥ DIRECTIONS ✥

✦ Add all the ingredients, except the hot water and garnish, to a rocks glass and stir. Add the hot water. Garnish with freshly grated nutmeg.

✥ INGREDIENTS ✥

¾ ounce Lapsang Souchong–Infused Old Forester Bourbon (see recipe at right)

½ ounce Lemon Sherbet (see page 71)

¼ ounce Smith & Cross Jamaican Rum

¼ ounce Banks 7 Rum

¼ ounce Cruzan Blackstrap Rum

¼ ounce Pimento Dram

2 dashes Dead Rabbit Orinoco Bitters or Angostura Aromatic Bitters

2 dashes Bittermens Xocolatl Mole Bitters

2 tablespoons butter, room temperature

3 ounces hot water

Fresh nutmeg, grated, for garnish

LAPSANG SOUCHONG–INFUSED OLD FORESTER BOURBON

* Place the tea bags in a quart canning jar. Fill the jar with bourbon and seal it shut.

* After 1 hour, remove the tea bags. Due to the alcohol content, this infusion should last indefinitely at room temperature.

YIELDS *About 750ml*

2 bags lapsang souchong tea

750ml bottle Old Forester Bourbon

STONE FENCE

Inspiration: Jerry Thomas, *The Bar-Tender's Guide*, 1862

Perhaps the American republic's first mixed drink, the Stone Fence was being quaffed by revolutionaries before, during, and after the War of Independence. (Quite a lot of it was during.) And rightfully so, as the hearty concoction was originally hard cider with rum in it, which ought to make anyone reconsider how the world is put together. Over the years, as revolutionaries became statesmen, the drink was sissified a bit into bourbon and sweet (nonalcoholic) cider.

We aim to recapture the Stone Fence for citizen philosophers, so we turn to our radical brethren in the French Republic for this drink's rethinking. Subbing luminous Calvados for heavier rum or bourbon was an easy decision, and our cider is anything but nonalcoholic. The other glorious Gallic ingredients are Chartreuse and pear liqueur, plus the international symbol of transformation and revolt, Dead Rabbit Orinoco Bitters.

⚜ DIRECTIONS ⚜

✦ Add all the ingredients, except the Cidre Bouche and garnish, to a mixing glass. Fill with ice and stir until chilled. Add the Cidre Bouche to the glass and strain the mixture into an ice-filled wine glass. Twist the lemon peel over the glass to express the oils, then discard the peel.

⚜ INGREDIENTS ⚜

3 dashes Dead Rabbit Orinoco Bitters or Angostura Aromatic Bitters

¾ ounce Merlet Crème de Poire

½ ounce Green Chartreuse

1½ ounces Château du Breuil VSOP Calvados

3 ounces Christian Drouin Cidre Bouche

Lemon peel, for garnish

PARISIAN

Inspiration: J. A. Grohusko, *Jack's Manual of Recipes for Fancy Mixed Drinks and How to Serve Them*, 1908

On the previous page we made a quintessentially American drink French. Now let's make a French drink *even more French*. In Jacob "Jack" Grohusko's formulation, this drink was Byrrh liqueur, a bit of lime juice, and soda water—a kind of Byrrh rickey. Hardly in step with the highly fashionable Parisians of the era. Let's festoon this glass instead with the exciting Cidre Bouche, which will bring orchard-mate Calvados along for a stronger foundation.

This has been transformed into a sibling of the Stone Fence, yet one which is both fruitier and more herbal. With its black currant and effervescence, you might suggest it for fans of the Kir Royale.

DIRECTIONS

+ Add all the ingredients, except the Cidre Bouche and garnish, to a mixing glass. Fill with ice and stir until chilled. Add the Cidre Bouche to the glass and strain the mixture into an ice-filled wine glass. Twist the lemon peel over the glass to express the oils, then discard the peel.

INGREDIENTS

3 dashes Bittermens Burlesque Bitters

¼ ounce Combier Crème de Cassis

1½ ounces Byrrh Grand Quinquina

1½ ounces Château du Breuil VSOP Calvados

3 ounces Christian Drouin Cidre Bouche

Lemon peel, for garnish

MASSAGRAND

Inspiration: Louis Muckensturm, *Louis' Mixed Drinks*, 1906

When Jack first read Muckensturm's recipe, he was reminded of the famed Café Brûlot, a postprandial staple of the grand French-Creole restaurants of New Orleans. Consisting of coffee, spices, sugar, and cognac, that drink is ignited tableside and ladled from a silver bowl.

The Massagrand has similar constituents, but is not intended to combust. The flavor structure is the same, but with stone fruit notes from eaux de vie and liqueurs, plus calamus, an interesting botanical that combines the qualities of cinnamon, nutmeg, and ginger.

If espresso for caffè americano is not available, your favorite strong coffee will do.

❖DIRECTIONS❖

✦ Fill one shaker with ice. Fill a second shaker with all the ingredients except the garnishes. Roll between the two shakers seven times, or until chilled (see note below). Strain into an ice-filled wine glass. Garnish with freshly grated nutmeg. Twist the orange peel over the glass to express the oils, then discard the peel.

✦ *A note on rolling: This is a simple technique meant to quickly chill drinks with less dilution from melted ice. All it means is to start with one iced shaker and one shaker with the drink ingredients. First you pour the ingredient shaker into the ice shaker. Then you pour the combined contents into the other shaker. Then you do it back again. Jack says seven times will be enough.*

❖INGREDIENTS❖

2 dashes Calamus Tincture (see page 195)

2 dashes Dead Rabbit Orinoco Bitters or Angostura Aromatic Bitters

1½ ounces caffè americano

½ ounce Cherry Heering

½ ounce F. Meyer Kirsch Eau de Vie

½ ounce F. Meyer Mirabelle Eau de Vie

1½ ounces Louis Royer VSOP Cognac

Fresh nutmeg, grated, for garnish

Orange peel, for garnish

CALAMUS TINCTURE

* Combine the calamus and Everclear in a jar. Allow to macerate for 3 days, then strain through a chinois into a fresh container. Add the water. Due to the alcohol content, this tincture should last indefinitely at room temperature.

1 ounce powdered calamus root

4½ ounces Everclear

4½ ounces water

YIELDS *About 750ml*

ICE CREAM SODA

We have updated the sling for the age of the soda fountain; never mind that that age is also far behind us. This creamy treat does indeed taste like its namesake, but with delicate stone fruit flavors hovering in the background.

Throughout his book, Fouquet again and again employs crème de noyaux, a liqueur made from the stones of apricots (not be confused with crème de noix, made from whole nuts, often walnuts). We're switching in two kinds of apricot liqueur instead for a bolder expression of that fruit.

DIRECTIONS

✦ Add all the ingredients, except the soda and garnish, to a shaker. Fill with ice and shake. Strain into an ice-filled wine glass. Add the soda and garnish with freshly grated nutmeg.

INGREDIENTS

½ ounce Vanilla Syrup (see page 123)

2 dashes Dead Rabbit Orinoco Bitters or Angostura Aromatic Bitters

1½ ounces half and half

¾ ounce Marie Brizard Apry

1 ounce F. Meyer Kirsch Eau de Vie

1 ounce Blume Marillen Apricot Eau de Vie

2 ounces soda water

Fresh nutmeg, grated, for garnish

AUTOMOBILE

Inspiration: Tim Daly, *Daly's Bartenders' Encyclopedia*, 1903

Daly's drink, which he mentions as being his own "very latest" creation, is essentially a variant Champagne cocktail, featuring dashes of aromatic bitters, curaçao, and Crème Yvette (a brand of parfait amour) in a tall glass of bubbly.

Jack was inspired by the original recipe but preferred to take it the direction of the infamous absinthe-and-Champagne concoction Death in the Afternoon (purportedly devised, like the book of the same name, by Ernest Hemingway). With absinthe as the new ground floor for this cocktail, other vegetal flavors suggested themselves, and finally we arrived at the vigorous combination listed below. Vibrant Champagne holds the disparate floral, citrus, and vegetal components in harmony.

We think this drink may someday be all the rage, like the horseless carriage, or "automobile."

·❊·DIRECTIONS·❊·

✦ Add all the ingredients, except the Piper Heidsieck and garnish, to a mixing glass. Fill with ice and stir until chilled. Add the Piper Heidsieck to the glass and strain the mixture into an ice-filled wine glass. Twist the lemon peel over the glass to express the oils, then discard the peel.

·❊·INGREDIENTS·❊·

½ ounce Celery Cordial (see page 198)

3 dashes Bittermens Orchard Street Celery Shrub

½ ounce Marie Brizard Parfait Amour

1 ounce Pernod Absinthe

3 ounces Piper-Heidsieck Cuvée Brut

Lemon peel, for garnish

CELERY CORDIAL

* Cut the celery stalks into chunks and feed them into a juice extractor.

* In a small saucepan, combine the juice, water, and sugar over medium heat, but do not boil. Slowly stir to dissolve the sugar. When the syrup has thickened, remove from the heat. Strain through a chinois into bottles. The cordial will keep for 2 to 3 weeks in the refrigerator.

YIELDS *About 20 ounces*

8 ounces celery

4 cups water

4 cups granulated sugar

FLIPS, POSSETS, AND NOGS

To make these drinks, we must raid the henhouse, for these three categories involve eggs. Do not fear them! Eggs are an essential ingredient in the kitchen, and in a proper bar they are another tool in the toolbox.

A flip involves spirit, sugar, and an egg. A nog encompasses those three ingredients, plus cream. The posset, an ancestor to both styles, was a spiced combination of milk and ale or wine, often with eggs. Although it was not always the case, starting in the twentieth century all would be served cold.

Note that when we say egg, we mean yellow and white, everything that's inside the shell. This adds a richness to the drinks that mere egg white cannot. Some people are concerned that adding eggs to drinks would make them taste like omelets, but those people must make terrible omelets. A closer approximation would be the central role eggs play in baking. These drinks are a bit like pastries that don't have to go in the oven.

PORTERBERRY

Inspiration: William Terrington, *Cooling Cups and Dainty Drinks*, 1869

The Aleberry is an ancient English drink involving ale, milk, toasted bread, and oatmeal. For those who were worried that adding eggs to drinks might make them taste like breakfast, please note that we're doing away with toast, oatmeal, and eggs in our Porterberry, which is not to say that it isn't still part of a balanced breakfast.

Instead of the bakery, we'll turn to the brewery, and choose a rich porter style of beer to replace the milder ale. Nowadays, brewers create porters with flavors as varied as pumpkin, chocolate, plum, and bourbon, so we're sure it can hold its own here. And to give this drink the kiss of dairy without drowning it in milk, we'll use just a teaspoon of butter. The butter also acts a bit like the egg would to bind things together—so after all the talk in the introduction about eggs, here's a place they weren't needed after all.

The term "flip" once had a different meaning within the beverage arts, and it's this extinct form that Jack was inspired by in creating the Porterberry. The first flip was an American tavern drink where a bowl would be filled with molasses, beer, spices, and rum, into which the barkeep would plunge a red-hot iron (or "flip-dog," apparently).

We're using Pusser's old-style rum for its strong molasses hit, plus porter and spices, but as we could not find a reliable source of flip-dogs, the Porterberry is served cold.

❋ DIRECTIONS ❋

✦ Add all the ingredients, except the garnishes, to a shaker. Fill with ice and shake. Strain into a wine glass. Garnish with freshly grated nutmeg. Twist the lemon peel over the glass to express the oils, then discard the peel.

❋ INGREDIENTS ❋

½ ounce Vanilla Syrup (see page 123)

2 dashes Dead Rabbit Orinoco Bitters or Angostura Aromatic Bitters

1 teaspoon butter, at room temperature

½ ounce Liquore Strega

¾ ounce fresh lemon juice

1½ ounces Founders Porter

1½ ounces Bowmore 12 Year Old Scotch Whiskey

1½ ounces Pusser's Navy Rum

Fresh nutmeg, grated, for garnish

Lemon peel, for garnish

GENERAL HARRISON

The tale of this drink spans centuries; it begins in 1839 and involves a future president of the United States. Later we'll get to the really important part, what Dale "King Cocktail" DeGroff did with the drink 150 years later.

William Henry Harrison was governor of the Indiana Territory, where he made his name by presiding over the Battle of Tippecanoe against Shawnee leader Tecumseh in 1811. Subsequent successes in the War of 1812 made him a national hero, but he retired to his farm in Ohio to grow corn. He built a whiskey distillery, but shortly "perceived the injurious effects resulting from such manufactories, and abolished his distillery; thus setting a bright and useful example to those around him, sacrificing his own pecuniary interest to the good of the community" (Samuel Jones Burr, *The Life and Times of William Henry Harrison*, 1840, p. 258). In 1836 he was a Whig candidate for the presidency, but was defeated by Democrat Martin Van Buren.

In December 1839, both men were nominated by their parties for a rematch in 1840. Almost immediately, a pro-Van Buren letter to the *Baltimore Republican* (December 11, 1839) dismissed the frontiersman as a rustic too simple-minded for important office: "Give him a barrel of hard cider and a pension of two thousand a year, and, our word for it, he will sit the remainder of his days in a log cabin." In the words of one Harrison campaigner, "There was nothing gross or very abusive in this sentence, but it very possibly carried the election" (Richard Smith Elliott, *Notes Taken in Sixty Years*, 1883, p. 121).

Instead of arguing against the characterization, Harrison supporters reveled in it. They promoted their man as a back-to-basics, true American who was proud of simple, honest things like farms, cabins, and cider. They wanted nothing to do with moneyed snobs of the Eastern Establishment like Van Buren. Of course, Martin Van Buren grew up poor in rural New York, and Harrison had been raised in luxury by a family involved in American politics since colonial days. And as we see, Harrison in fact shunned alcohol as sinful. This information did not clutter the narrative.

"Hard cider became almost the sole beverage of the Whigs throughout the country. In every city, town and village, and at the cross-roads, were erected log-cabins, while the amount of hard cider drunk would have floated the American Navy" (*The Voter's Guide to the Campaign of 1900*, Charles Morris, Edward Sylvester Ellis, and Isaac Thorne Johnson, 1900, pp. 49–50). Harrison won the election.

Today, Harrison is probably best remembered for being the president with the longest inaugural address but shortest term of office, as he died thirty days after making his speech. It has long been said that the cause of death was pneumonia, but modern research suggests that the real cause was bacterial infection from contaminated water. "In those days the nation's capital had no sewer system. Until 1850, some sewage simply flowed onto public grounds a short distance from the White House, where it stagnated and formed a marsh; the White House water supply was just seven blocks downstream of a depository for 'night soil,' hauled there each day at government expense" (Jane McHugh and Philip A. Mackowiak, "What Really Killed William Henry Harrison?", *The New York Times*, April 1, 2014, p. D3).

So, Harrison should have stuck to cider.

Jerry Thomas honors the man in his 1862 guide with "General Harrison's Egg Nogg." It removes the cream and the bourbon we associate with eggnog and replaces them with the famous cider. (It is also notable that the drink is to commemorate the beloved "General Harrison" and not his later incarnation as the ephemeral "President Harrison.")

An eggnog based on cider is a terrific idea; removing the ingredients that make it recognizable as an eggnog, though, is somewhat troubling. That modern descendent of Professor Thomas, Dale DeGroff, decided that the drink could handle both cider and bourbon, which is how he describes it in his 2008 book *The Essential Cocktail*.

When it became Jack's turn to consider the recipe, he finished the restoration by putting the cream back as well. Now we have a proper eggnog exhibiting all its fine characteristics of cream, egg, and powerful liquor, but yet wonderfully light due to its basis in cider. And chalk up a late win for the snob aesthetes, as this cider's French.

DIRECTIONS

+ Add all the ingredients, except the Christian Drouin Cidre Bouche and garnish, to a shaker and shake. Add ice and shake again vigorously. Add the Christian Drouin Cidre Bouche. Strain into a wine glass and garnish with freshly grated nutmeg.

INGREDIENTS

1¼ ounces Spiced Sugar Syrup (see recipe below)

2 dashes Allspice Tincture (see page 123)

1 large egg

2 dashes Dead Rabbit Orinoco Bitters or Angostura Aromatic Bitters

1½ ounces half-and-half

2 ounces Woodford Reserve Bourbon

2 ounces Bulleit Bourbon

2½ ounces Christian Drouin Cidre Bouche

Fresh nutmeg, grated, for garnish

SPICED SUGAR SYRUP

+ Combine the sugar and water in a medium saucepan over medium heat, but do not boil. Add the spices and slowly stir to dissolve the sugar. When the syrup has thickened, remove from the heat. Strain through a chinois into bottles. The syrup will keep for 2 to 3 weeks in the refrigerator.

YIELDS *About 16 ounces*

2 cups granulated sugar

2 cups water

1 teaspoon ground star anise

½ teaspoon ground allspice

½ teaspoon ground cloves

1 teaspoon ground mace

1 teaspoon grated nutmeg

¼ teaspoon ground cinnamon

ALE FLIP

Inspiration: Jerry Thomas, *The Bar-Tender's Guide*, 1862

Thomas' Ale Flip was a warm, spiced remedy for a cold. We'll combine a medley of tinctures, bitters, and liqueurs to bring the spice, and let Powers whiskey provide the warmth.

While Thomas delineates a Rum Flip, where rum is added to the beer, and notes the same for brandy, he includes no flip with whiskey. We have corrected this oversight. Contrasting the strong malty notes of the whiskey and ale is the hazelnut undertone from Suze. Altogether an autumnal beverage, rich and unusual.

DIRECTIONS

+ Add all the ingredients, except the garnish, to a shaker and shake. Add ice and shake again vigorously. Strain into a wine glass and garnish with freshly grated nutmeg.

INGREDIENTS

1 ounce Spiced Sugar Syrup (see page 207)

2 dashes Allspice Tincture (see page 123)

2 dashes Dead Rabbit Orinoco Bitters or Angostura Aromatic Bitters

1 large egg

¼ ounce Suze Gentiane

1½ ounces Powers Irish Whiskey

1½ ounces cask ale

Fresh nutmeg, grated, for garnish

BALTIMORE EGGNOG

Inspiration: E. Ricket and C. Thomas, *The Gentleman's Table Guide*, 1871

The generally accepted recipe for a Baltimore Eggnog starts with Madeira, cognac, and Jamaican rum—but E. Ricket and C. Thomas were not on this planet to go along with every popular notion. They decommissioned cognac in favor of Irish whiskey and traded Madeira for its brighter cousin sherry.

In that formulation, the malt nuances of the whiskey integrate with the raisin tone from the Pedro Ximénez sherry, the vanilla syrup, and the molasses notes from the blend of rums. It makes for an extra-special nog indeed.

DIRECTIONS

+ Add all the ingredients, except the garnish, to a shaker and shake. Add ice and shake again vigorously. Strain into a wine glass and garnish with freshly grated nutmeg.

INGREDIENTS

½ ounce Vanilla Syrup (see page 123)

1 large egg

1½ ounces half-and-half

⅓ ounce Smith & Cross Jamaican Rum

⅓ ounce Banks 7 Rum

⅓ ounce Cruzan Blackstrap Rum

1½ ounces Jameson 12 Year Old Irish Whiskey

1 ounce Hidalgo Pedro Ximénez Sherry

Fresh nutmeg, grated, for garnish

CAFÉ ROYAL

Inspiration: William T. Boothby, *Cocktail Boothby's American Bartender*, 1891

Boothby's creation is a cup of hot coffee into which a flaming, Chartreuse-soaked sugar cube is descended. Points for style, but we can take it further.

Jack's flip interpretation uses coffee-flavored Galliano Ristretto plus two more intriguing herbal liqueurs featuring mint and rue. Rue imparts a musky pungency not entirely unlike wet hay, and is sometimes used to flavor cream cheese and game meat.

❖ DIRECTIONS ❖

✦ Add all the ingredients, except the garnish, to a shaker and shake. Add ice and shake again vigorously. Strain into a wine glass and garnish with freshly grated nutmeg.

❖ INGREDIENTS ❖

2 dashes Eucalyptus Tincture (see page 75)

1 large egg

½ ounce Nardini Aquavite di Vinaccia Rue Flavored Grappa

½ ounce Fernet Branca Menta

¾ ounce Galliano Ristretto

1 ounce Green Chartreuse

Fresh nutmeg, grated, for garnish

MULLED
EGG-WINE

Inspiration: William Terrington, *Cooling Cups and Dainty Drinks*, 1869

And now, a posset. Never before attempted on stage or bar! Or certainly not for a very, very long time.

Posset history goes back to the fifteenth century, when the English made them from hot milk curdled by wine or ale. By the sixteenth century, cream, sugar, and eggs were used instead, and citrus did the curdling. In our Mulled Egg-Wine, a kind of universal posset appropriate to any occasion, elements of both periods are shown.

Once, possets were so central to epicurean life that "posset sets" for serving them were common gifts. One assembled from crystal, gold, and precious gems and gifted to Queen Mary I of England by King Philip II of Spain on their betrothal is still on display in Hatfield House. Check your attics.

Our version, however, is not curdled, and the lemon component has been reigned in to just the peels. But whether or not you have a posset set to serve it in, it's a proud beverage in your repertoire from centuries past.

❧ DIRECTIONS ❧

✦ Prepare an oleo-saccharum with the lemon peels and sugar (see page 64).

✦ Combine all the ingredients, except the garnish, in a large mixing bowl and mix with a handheld blender. Pour into sherry glasses (or posset cups) and garnish with freshly grated nutmeg.

YIELDS *4 servings*

❧ INGREDIENTS ❧

3 lemons

⅜ cup superfine sugar

1 cup Spice Mixture (see page 214)

3 dashes Dead Rabbit Orinoco Bitters or Angostura Aromatic Bitters

2 large eggs

8½ ounces Barbadillo "Obispo Gascon" Palo Cortado Sherry

Fresh nutmeg, grated, for garnish

SPICE MIXTURE

* Boil the water and add the spices. Allow to simmer until the liquid has been reduced to 1 cup. Strain through a chinois before using.

YIELDS *About 1 cup*

1⅓ cups water

¼ teaspoon ground cardamom

¼ teaspoon ground cloves

⅛ teaspoon ground allspice

1½ teaspoons ground star anise

¼ teaspoon ground mace

½ teaspoon ground cinnamon

BISHOPS

E arlier, we explored cups and cobblers, which combined wines with herbaceous flavors. Bishops are also wine-based, but with a preference for the spicy.

Spiced wine may be the original mixed drink, as it was in use by the ancient Egyptians and is mentioned throughout classical Roman texts. By the Middle Ages, it seems every up-and-coming European nation had its take on the category, including *vin chaud* in France, *Glühwein* in Germany, Italian *vin brulé*, Polish *grzane wino*, Hungarian *forralt bor*, *vin fiert* from Romania, and Dutch *bisschopswijn*. In each language, the name refers to heating, boiling, cooking, or burning wine—except the Dutch term, "bishop's wine." While theories abound, there's no clear connection between hot wine and bishopry, though the term found its way into English as well.

The British in particular love spiced wine, and kept creating new versions of it from medieval through Victorian times. The examples we'll see in this chapter largely come from English and British tradition, usually served in the winter festive season. As we advocate year-round celebration, we've included optional modifications to many of the hot drinks to cool them for summer utility as well.

ARCHBISHOP

Inspiration: E. Ricket and C. Thomas, *The Gentleman's Table Guide*, 1871

Substitute the workaday wine of a bishop with magical port, and you have an Archbishop. (Actually, some chroniclers put it the other way, but we think that port brings one closer to heaven.) This is a very elegant spiced wine indeed, and was the classic English hot punch in the Victorian era, doled out to celebrate the festive season leading up to Christmas.

But there's no reason that these spiced wines need to be locked away until wintertime, so Jack has devised entirely ahistorical summertime editions. These versions start with the same basic mix, and with a few tweaks, your winter warmer becomes a primal sangría for beachfront or balcony. Both seasonal versions are explained below.

DIRECTIONS

WINTER EDITION

* Warm the Archbishop Mix in a small saucepan and pour into a wine glass. Garnish with freshly grated nutmeg. Twist the lemon peel over the glass to express the oils, then discard the peel. Do the same with the orange peel.

SUMMER EDITION

* Add all the ingredients, except the garnishes, to a shaker. Fill with ice and shake. Strain into a wine glass. Garnish with freshly grated nutmeg. Twist the lemon peel over the glass to express the oils, then discard the peel. Do the same with the orange peel.

INGREDIENTS

5 ounces Archbishop Mix (see page 220)

Fresh nutmeg, grated, for garnish

Lemon peel, for garnish

Orange peel, for garnish

5 ounces Archbishop Mix (see page 220)

1 teaspoon fresh lemon juice

1 teaspoon orange juice

1 teaspoon Graham's LBV

½ ounce Remy Martin 1738 Cognac

Fresh nutmeg, grated, for garnish

Lemon peel, for garnish

Orange peel, for garnish

ARCHBISHOP MIX

✦ Combine all the ingredients in a 16-ounce jar. Allow to macerate for 3 days, then strain through a chinois into a fresh container. Due to the alcohol content, this mix should last indefinitely at room temperature.

YIELDS *About 12 ounces*

¾ ounce Ginger Syrup (see page 118)

Zest of 1 orange

Pinch ground mace

1 teaspoon brown sugar

1 teaspoon ground cinnamon

½ teaspoon ground cloves

½ teaspoon ground allspice

3 ounces Cherry Heering

8 ounces port

LAWN SLEEVES

Inspiration: Richard Cook, *Oxford Night Caps*, 1835

Cook believes that the ecclesiastical nomenclature of the spiced wine family derives from "the circumstance of ancient dignitaries of the Church, when they honoured the University with a visit, being regaled with spiced wine." In a book called *Oxford Night Caps*, such a view would certainly harmonize.

Whether or not we accept Oxford as the font from which these beverages originally flowed, Cook makes an important contribution to their taxonomy. Rather than being a single species, the bishops are a genus: The Pope is made with Burgundy, the Cardinal with Champagne, and finally the Lawn Sleeves with Madeira.

"Lawn Sleeves" is itself a reference to the bishops of Anglican or Roman Catholic persuasion, as their ceremonial garments had sleeves of finest linen from Laon, a town in France known for such work. Our Lawn Sleeves is perfumed by mace and sarsaparilla, its wintry portrayal similar to the Excellent Negus (see page 231), while its summer face may remind one of a refreshing Sherry Cobbler.

❋ DIRECTIONS ❋

WINTER EDITION

✦ Warm the Lawn Sleeves Mix in a small saucepan and pour into a wine glass. Garnish with freshly grated nutmeg. Twist the lemon peel over the glass to express the oils, then discard the peel.

SUMMER EDITION

✦ Add all the ingredients, except the garnishes, to a shaker. Fill with ice and shake. Strain into a wine glass. Garnish with freshly grated nutmeg. Twist the lemon peel over the glass to express the oils, then discard the peel.

❋ INGREDIENTS ❋

5 ounces Lawn Sleeves Mix (see page 222)

Fresh nutmeg, grated, for garnish

Lemon peel, for garnish

5 ounces Lawn Sleeves Mix (see page 222)

1 teaspoon fresh lemon juice

1 teaspoon Cossart Gordon 5 Year Old Bual Madeira

½ ounce Remy Martin 1738 Cognac

Fresh nutmeg, grated, for garnish

Lemon peel, for garnish

LAWN SLEEVES MIX

* Combine all the ingredients in a 16-ounce jar. Allow to macerate for 3 days, then strain through a chinois into a fresh container. Due to the alcohol content, this mix should last indefinitely at room temperature.

YIELDS *About 14 ounces*

2 dashes Terra Firma Sarsaparilla Tincture

Zest of 1 lemon

¾ teaspoon ground cloves

¾ teaspoon ground allspice

Pinch ground mace

⅛ cup brown sugar

1 ounce fresh lemon juice

12 ounces Madeira

NEW YORK RAISER

Inspiration: Louis Muckensturm, *Louis' Mixed Drinks*, 1906

Featuring sparkling wine and sweet sherbet, the New York Raiser could be considered akin to a Champagne Cobbler. Involving bitters, too, though, it might be compared to a Champagne Cocktail. But this is New York, after all; can't we have both?

Compared with the ancient mulled wines in this category, it's simple in both execution and composition. In our spiced wine category, the New York Raiser is the only sparkling example; it's also the lightest and the driest, making it an excellent palate cleanser or apéritif.

DIRECTIONS

+ Add all the ingredients, except the garnish, to a mixing glass. Fill with ice and stir until chilled. Strain into a wine glass with one chunk of cracked ice. Garnish with freshly grated nutmeg. Twist the lemon peel over the glass to express the oils, then discard the peel.

INGREDIENTS

¾ ounce Lemon Sherbet (see page 71)

2 dashes Dead Rabbit Orinoco Bitters or Angostura Aromatic Bitters

4 ounces Crémant de Limoux Wine

Fresh nutmeg, grated, for garnish

Lemon peel, for garnish

ALYMETH

Inspiration: William Schmidt, *The Flowing Bowl*, 1892

Another relatively recent American contribution, Schmidt's Alymeth is casually placed in his punch chapter despite its obvious connections to the bishop tradition. Of course, if you devise a new drink every day, as Schmidt was purported to have done, categories may begin to lose their significance.

This is the most herbal bishop we are putting forward, anchored with bay leaf, anise, and coriander. It's an earthy beverage for serious occasions.

❧ DIRECTIONS ❧

WINTER EDITION

✦ Warm the Alymeth Mix in a small saucepan and pour into a wine glass. Garnish with freshly grated nutmeg. Twist the lemon peel over the glass to express the oils, then discard the peel. Do the same with the orange peel.

SUMMER EDITION

✦ Add all the ingredients, except the garnishes, to a shaker. Fill with ice and shake. Strain into a wine glass. Garnish with freshly grated nutmeg. Twist the lemon peel over the glass to express the oils, then discard the peel. Do the same with the orange peel.

❧ INGREDIENTS ❧

5 ounces Alymeth Mix (see recipe at right)

Fresh nutmeg, grated, for garnish

Lemon peel, for garnish

Orange peel, for garnish

5 ounces Alymeth Mix (see recipe at right)

1 teaspoon fresh lemon juice

1 teaspoon orange juice

½ ounce Remy Martin 1738 Cognac

½ ounce red Burgundy

Fresh nutmeg, grated, for garnish

Lemon peel, for garnish

Orange peel, for garnish

ALYMETH MIX

✦ Combine all the ingredients in a 16-ounce jar. Allow to macerate for 3 days, then strain through a chinois into a fresh container. Due to the alcohol content, this mix should last indefinitely at room temperature.

YIELDS *About 14 ounces*

Zest of 1 orange

¼ cup brown sugar

1 ounce orange juice

¼ teaspoon ground cardamom

¼ teaspoon ground star anise

1 teaspoon ground coriander

1 dried bay leaf

12 ounces red Burgundy

LAMB'S WOOL

Inspiration: Robert Herrick, *Twelfe-Night, or King and Queene*, 1648

The label "Lamb's Wool" is thought to have come via the ancient Celtic pagan festival of *La Mas Ubal*, or the Day of the Apple. The drink consists of roasted apples, sugar, nutmeg, ginger, and quite a lot of strong ale, in quantities sufficient for a party of thirsty wassailers.

The practice of wassailing, thought to have originated in the West of England before the Norman conquest, is an antecedent of Christmas caroling, trick-or-treating, and mob riot. The term comes from the Middle English *waes hael* (good health)—a toast. But the toast could be one-sided. Bands of peasants trekked through the countryside and, coming upon a noble's house, would burst into song until they were given refreshment. If they were not given it, they would keep singing. Is all this good cheer or a threat?

Less menacing is the form of wassailing directed toward orchards rather than alms. To promote productive growth of their trees, the community would join together to sing pro-arboreal anthems, and, while they were there, hoist a few glasses of those trees' noble cider produce.

Robert Herrick's seventeenth-century poem concerns itself with baking for the last day of Christmas, and makes clear that a bowl of Lamb's Wool is not to be omitted from the day's catering:

> Next crowne the bowle full
> With gentle Lambs wool,
>   Adde sugar, nutmeg, and ginger,
> With store of ale too,
> And thus ye must doe
>   To make the Wassaile a swinger.

In Jack's imagination, the Lamb's Wool has been transformed into a baked apple floating on a whiskey sea. This should only be served hot, as a West Country answer to the Irish Coffee or Whiskey Toddy.

And while we may all from time to time desire a proper cup of coffee from a proper copper coffeepot, Jack has determined that no modern wassailist should be without a traditional metal Greek coffeepot, or *briki*. The *briki* is used to heat coffee (and, now, the Lamb's Wool) directly over a burner. Give it a try and cement Hellenic-Somerset relations.

+ Combine all the ingredients, except the garnish, in a *briki*. Place the *briki* on a burner and heat to a boil. When bubbling hot, pour into a porcelain mug and garnish with freshly grated nutmeg.

3 ounces Spiced Apple Purée (see recipe below)

½ ounce Spiced Sugar Syrup (see page 207)

4 ounces Founders Porter

2 ounces Powers Irish Whiskey

Fresh nutmeg, grated, for garnish

SPICED APPLE PURÉE

+ Add all the ingredients to a jar and mix. The purée should last two weeks in the refrigerator.

YIELDS *About 10 ounces*

4 ounces Ginger Syrup (see page 118)

4 ounces applesauce, store-bought or homemade

¼ ounce Everclear

EXCELLENT NEGUS

Inspiration: William Terrington, *Cooling Cups and Dainty Drinks*, 1869

Before there was the Fourth Earl of Sandwich, there was Colonel Francis Negus, member of Parliament for Ipswich, who likewise gave his name to a concoction of the dining table. According to legend, when wine was running out during a heated political discussion one evening, Negus suggested lengthening the supplies with sugar and hot water. This solution was so welcomed that all those assembled lost track of their political differences and began to discuss the merits of the drink instead.

Of course, since the bishop style of wine presentation was already well known by the early eighteenth century when this was meant to be happening, it's possible that Negus was merely advocating the watering down of an already spiced wine. Nonetheless, recipes with his name persist, and this is a delicious one—a kind of light sherry punch. Try it with sandwiches!

❖ DIRECTIONS ❖

WINTER EDITION

+ Warm the Excellent Negus Mix in a small saucepan and pour into a wine glass. Garnish with freshly grated nutmeg. Twist the lemon peel over the glass to express the oils, then discard the peel. Do the same with the orange peel.

SUMMER EDITION

+ Add all the ingredients, except the garnishes, to a shaker. Fill with ice and shake. Strain into a wine glass. Garnish with freshly grated nutmeg. Twist the lemon peel over the glass to express the oils, then discard the peel.

❖ INGREDIENTS ❖

6 ounces Excellent Negus Mix (see page 232)

Fresh nutmeg, grated, for garnish

Lemon peel, for garnish

Orange peel, for garnish

5 ounces Excellent Negus Mix (see page 232)

1 teaspoon fresh lemon juice

½ ounce oloroso sherry

Fresh nutmeg, grated, for garnish

Lemon peel, for garnish

EXCELLENT NEGUS MIX

✦ Combine all the ingredients in a 16-ounce jar. Allow to macerate for 3 days, then strain through a chinois into a fresh container. Due to the alcohol content, this mix should last indefinitely at room temperature.

YIELDS *About 15 ounces*

½ ounce Vanilla Syrup (see page 123)

Zest of 2 lemons

4 ounces water

¼ cup superfine sugar

2 ounces fresh lemon juice

7 ounces oloroso sherry

2 ounces cognac

1 teaspoon grated nutmeg

COCKTAILS

First of all, let it be known that "cocktail" is a silly word. The reason it was originally used to refer to a certain type of mixed drink (or, indeed, in contemporary usage, to mean any mixed drink) is not known; there are many amusing stories purporting to reveal its etymology, and every drink book dutifully lists them, but while many can be disproved, none can be proved. So we are stuck with this absurd-sounding word of no known origin. Fortunately, things can be bigger than their names.

The first usage of "cocktail" to mean a mixed drink is also not clear, with some recent scholarship suggesting it may have originated in London in the 1790s, and other scholarship suggesting that is a dirty lie borne of anti-Americanism. But nonetheless we were supplied with a handy definition in *The Balance and Columbian Repository of Hudson*, New York, on Tuesday, May 13, 1806, in the reply to a letter to the editor. Harry Croswell, editor, explained that "Cock-tail is a stimulating liquor, composed of spirits of any kind, sugar, water, and bitters—it is vulgarly called bittered sling," before going on to do his intended editorial work: ". . . and is supposed to be an excellent electioneering potion, inasmuch as it renders the heart stout and bold, at the same time that it fuddles the head. It is said, also to be of great use to a democratic candidate: because a person, having swallowed a glass of it, is ready to swallow any thing else."

So the very first known description of the cocktail takes the opportunity to include sarcastic political commentary in an Ambrose Bierce-like witty definition. We consider this an auspicious start.

But let us to return to "spirits of any kind, sugar, water, and bitters." That also sounds like a good place to start. In fact, it sounds like an Old Fashioned, Sazerac, or other ancient iced drinks. By the time of Jerry Thomas, who included cocktails in his *Bar-Tender's Guide*, cocktails were more normally served up, being diluted in stirring with ice rather than with the addition of water or ice to the glass.

That is how we will approach the category, as stirred drinks with a heavy spirit component, and sweetening and bittering agents. No juice is involved. In fact, our cocktails tend to be on the dry side. These are apéritifs that will showcase the spirits involved. Turn to another chapter for your after-dinner needs.

Finally, after almost an entire book, we present the cocktail, often considered the pinnacle of mixed drink achievement. Hope you're thirsty.

GLEE CLUB

Inspiration: Tim Daly, *Daly's Bartenders' Encyclopedia*, 1903

A 1903 cocktail known as the Glee Club may sound stuck in its time. But don your straw boater and give it a chance. This version of the drink is Jack's amalgamation of Daly's Glee Club with two similar drinks of the same period, the Vermouth Cocktail and the Bamboo. Both of the latter drinks involve sherry, but rather than combine sherry with vermouth, a second fortified wine, Jack has chosen to emphasize sherry. The Chartreuse and fruit flavors of the original Glee Club's recipe are included, though Jack is using dry eaux de vie rather than the original raspberry wine.

It's an excellent apéritif in three-part harmony. Our Glee Club is as clean as an undergraduate shirt front on the night of the big concert, and it celebrates one of our favorite underutilized cocktail components, sherry.

DIRECTIONS

* Add all the ingredients, except the garnish, to a mixing glass. Fill with ice and stir until chilled. Strain the mixture into a cocktail glass. Twist the lemon peel over the glass to express the oils, then discard the peel.

INGREDIENTS

3 dashes Pernod Absinthe

3 dashes Bittermens Burlesque Bitters

¾ ounce Yellow Chartreuse

½ ounce F. Meyer Framboise Eau de Vie

2½ ounces Barbadillo Amontillado Sherry

Lemon peel, for garnish

EAU DE THÉ COCKTAIL

Inspiration: Charles H. Baker, *The Gentleman's Companion*, 1939

Resplendent socialite Baker created the "Jimmie Roosevelt" by combining the world-beating trio of Chartreuse, cognac, and Champagne. We like it. But we never rest on our laurels, even when they are on the shoulders of giants. For our variation, we're perking it up a bit with our Eau de Thé Syrup, an herbal suffusion like no other.

If you are afraid of Chartreuse, this drink will strike terror to your soul. But if you have learned what bartenders have learned, that Chartreuse is just as afraid of you, then revel in this inspired solution. If you have not yet taken this lesson on board, the time for self-improvement is now. Chartreuse, in the right hands, is a force for good.

❖ DIRECTIONS ❖

✦ Add all the ingredients, except the Champagne and garnish, to a mixing glass. Fill with ice and stir until chilled. Strain the mixture into an ice-filled punch glass. Add the Champagne. Twist the orange peel over the glass to express the oils, then discard the peel.

❖ INGREDIENTS ❖

¼ ounce Eau de Thé Syrup (see page 80)

1½ ounces Remy Martin VSOP

½ ounce Green Chartreuse

3 dashes Dead Rabbit Orinoco Bitters or Angostura Aromatic Bitters

2 ounces brut Champagne

Orange peel, for garnish

ANGELUS

Inspiration: William Schmidt, *The Flowing Bowl*, 1892

In the 1890s, Martini-style cocktails were much stronger on vermouth than they would be decades later, when wags would joke about "waving the bottle" over otherwise unadulterated gin (or, if they were especially comedic, vodka). But this book is not about teaching you how to pour gin into a glass. It is about flavor, and while gin has it, vermouth has even more. (Just for good measure, so do the other four ingredients in the Angelus.)

When the Martini was first documented during the 1880s, it was essentially equal parts booze and fortified vermouth, with a teaspoon of cordial, some absinthe, and maybe bitters. Twenty years later, the dry Martini reigned supreme, with cordials, absinthe, and bitters altogether gone, and vermouth drying up into nothingness with each passing year.

Gum syrup, rather than simple sugar syrup, adds another dimension: texture. The round mouthfeel comes from the slightest hint of solidification into gum. Sometimes called by its French name, *gomme*, it isn't seen much today because of its more difficult and expensive process, but it's the luxurious sweetener you would have seen behind the best 1890s hotel bars.

So let us set the clock back and enjoy the Angelus, with the citric bite of Amère Nouvelle, the saffron-tinged Old Raj, and plenty of dry vermouth, in the style of our ancestors.

DIRECTIONS

⁺ Add all the ingredients, except the garnish, to a mixing glass. Fill with ice and stir until chilled. Strain the mixture into a cocktail glass. Twist the lemon peel over the glass to express the oils, then discard the peel.

INGREDIENTS

¼ ounce Gum Syrup (see recipe at right)

3 dashes Pernod Absinthe

1 dash orange bitters

½ ounce Bittermens Amère Nouvelle

1½ ounces Dolin Dry Vermouth

2 ounces Cadenhead's Old Raj Gin

Lemon peel, for garnish

GUM SYRUP

* In a small saucepan, heat 2 ounces of the water over medium heat, but do not boil. Add the gum arabic and slowly stir to dissolve. Allow this mixture to cool.

* Combine the sugar and remaining water in a medium saucepan over medium heat, but do not boil. Slowly stir to dissolve the sugar. Add the gum arabic mixture. Boil for 2 minutes, stirring constantly, then remove from the heat and allow to cool.

* Use a funnel to pour into bottles. The syrup will keep for 2 to 3 weeks in the refrigerator.

YIELDS *About 14 ounces*

2 ounces plus 2 cups water

2 ounces gum arabic

2 cups granulated sugar

MONTANA CLUB

Inspiration: J. A. Grohusko, *Jack's Manual of Recipes for Fancy Mixed Drinks and How to Serve Them*, 1908

If the Angelus (see page 240) is our house Martini style, then the Montana Club is our Manhattan. However, just as with the Glee Club (see page 236), as much as we appreciate and admire it, we're not wedded to vermouth as the only fortified wine.

So let us consider Bonal Gentiane, an exceptionally herbaceous mixture, in its place. And while we're at it, let's switch out whiskey for cognac (a Manhattan with cognac is sometimes called a Harvard, but we're making this drink for a different kind of club).

There are whole volumes on the Manhattan and its family. Spring the Montana Club on a world-weary Manhattan drinker—it will be new.

DIRECTIONS

✦ Add all the ingredients, except the garnish, to a mixing glass. Fill with ice and stir until chilled. Strain the mixture into a cocktail glass. Twist the lemon peel over the glass to express the oils, then discard the peel.

INGREDIENTS

2 dashes Dead Rabbit Orinoco Bitters or Angostura Aromatic Bitters

2 dashes Boker's Bitters

½ ounce Marie Brizard Anisette

¼ ounce Amaro Sibilla

1 ounce Bonal Gentiane

1½ ounces Louis Royer VSOP Cognac

Lemon peel, for garnish

HOLLAND GIN
À LA THOMAS

Inspiration: Jerry Thomas, *The Bar-Tenders' Guide*, 1876

The 1876 reissue of Professor Thomas' guide included an appendix of drinks "improved" since the previous edition. We will keep the tradition running and "improve" one of those in turn.

Ours is a softer, perhaps more accessible, iteration of Thomas' Improved Holland Gin Cocktail. No mistake, it's still extremely challenging even in its more forgiving state. But with the herbal rat-a-tat of Strega (pine), kümmel (caraway), Aveze (gentian), and Chartreuse (everything), we have moved the focus a bit from the astringent genever. This is an eye-opener indeed!

❈ DIRECTIONS ❈

✦ Add all the ingredients, except the garnish, to a mixing glass. Fill with ice and stir until chilled. Strain the mixture into a cocktail glass. Twist the orange peel over the glass to express the oils, then discard the peel.

❈ INGREDIENTS ❈

2 dashes Pernod Absinthe

2 dashes Peychaud's Bitters

2 dashes orange bitters

¼ ounce Liquore Strega

¼ ounce Combier Kümmel

½ ounce Yellow Chartreuse

½ ounce Aveze Gentiane

2½ ounces Bols Genever

Orange peel, for garnish

WHISKEY COCKTAIL

Inspiration: William Schmidt, *The Flowing Bowl*, 1892

Schmidt's original is heavily boozy, a whiskey and bitters brawler in the best cocktail tradition. As with many of the drinks in this chapter, we're taming the beast and evening out the flavors. For this recipe, we will ratchet up the bitters component with two complementary formulas, plus our old standby, absinthe. Further seasoning comes via gloriously herbal Bénédictine (perhaps familiar to most imbibers when combined with brandy as B&B) and Royal Combier, which is a spicy liqueur that has in fact already been blended into brandy.

Royal Combier, featuring aloe, nutmeg, myrrh, cardamom, cinnamon, and saffron, is a perfect foil to the nuttiness of Old Overholt. Bénédictine involves twenty-seven secret herbs and spices, far more than needed even for fried chicken. Nonetheless, fried chicken goes great with a Whiskey Cocktail.

⊰ DIRECTIONS ⊱

+ Add all the ingredients, except the garnish, to a mixing glass. Fill with ice and stir until chilled. Strain the mixture into a cocktail glass. Twist the orange peel over the glass to express the oils, then discard the peel.

⊰ INGREDIENTS ⊱

2 ounces Old Overholt Rye Whiskey

¾ ounce Bénédictine

¼ ounce Royal Combier

3 dashes Dead Rabbit Orinoco Bitters or Angostura Aromatic bitters

3 dashes orange bitters

3 dashes Pernod Absinthe

Orange peel, for garnish

IMPROVED IRISH WHISKEY COCKTAIL

Inspiration: Jerry Thomas, *The Bar-Tenders' Guide*, 1876

What should one drink to follow a Whiskey Cocktail? Obviously, if one wants to move ever forward, an Improved Whiskey Cocktail. Thomas never specifies the whiskey's nationality, so we'll improve on the Improved and say Irish.

Jameson Black Barrel Whiskey, a relatively new product, offers another hue on the bartender's palette. Aged in charred oak barrels like bourbon, it takes on more of the barrels' vanilla characteristics. But we'll preclude too sweet a drink with our favorite dry maraschino liqueur.

Combier Elisir is the spicy liqueur basis for Royal Combier, but without the brandy that would conflict with our whiskey. We're increasing our dependence on absinthe, as well, since that is the best definition of improvement.

DIRECTIONS

✦ Add all the ingredients, except the garnish, to a mixing glass. Fill with ice and stir until chilled. Strain the mixture into a cocktail glass. Twist the orange peel over the glass to express the oils, then discard the peel.

INGREDIENTS

2 ounces Jameson Black Barrel Irish Whiskey

½ ounce Combier Elisir

½ ounce maraschino liqueur

¼ ounce Pernod Absinthe

3 dashes orange bitters

3 dashes Peychaud's Bitters

Orange peel, for garnish

GLADSTONE

Inspiration: William Schmidt, *The Flowing Bowl*, 1892

Here is our Old Fashioned representative, back to the 1806 definition of the cocktail as "spirits of any kind, sugar, water, and bitters." We've frozen the water and multiplied the spirits. Since a proper Old Fashioned is made with good old rye, and rye can have a bready characteristic, let's emphasize that with aquavit's caraway basis (that seed you see stuck onto your loaf of rye bread) and sweetened with the *je ne sais quoi* of Parfait Amour. For mouthfeel there is the roundness of Gum Syrup rather than mere mortal sugar.

Keep a flaskful in your Gladstone bag. If William Schmidt could see us now!

DIRECTIONS

+ Add all the ingredients, except the garnish, to a mixing glass. Fill with ice and stir until chilled. Strain the mixture into a cocktail glass. Twist the lemon peel over the glass to express the oils, then discard the peel.

INGREDIENTS

¼ ounce Gum Syrup (see page 241)

3 dashes Pernod Absinthe

3 dashes Dead Rabbit Orinoco Bitters or Angostura Aromatic Bitters

½ ounce Parfait Amour

¾ ounce Aalborg Aquavit

2 ounces Rittenhouse Rye

Lemon peel, for garnish

HUNTER

Inspiration: J. A. Grohusko, *Jack's Manual of Recipes for Fancy Mixed Drinks and How to Serve Them*, 1908

The Hunter, as specified in *Jack's Manual* of 1908, is three-fourths rye and one-fourth cherry brandy. Our own Jack has run with those flavors to create this more nuanced version, using rye and a cherry liqueur but also several agents offering needed bitterness for balance.

This is a particularly good showcase for the rich and delicately spicy Bittermens Xocolatl Mole Bitters, an Aztec inspiration in the midst of the modern bar.

DIRECTIONS

• Add all the ingredients, except the garnish, to a mixing glass. Fill with ice and stir until chilled. Strain the mixture into a cocktail glass. Twist the orange peel over the glass to express the oils, then discard the peel.

INGREDIENTS

2 ounces Bulleit Rye

¾ ounce The Bitter Truth EXR Amaro

½ ounce Combier Roi Rene Rouge Cherry Liqueur

¼ ounce Pernod Absinthe

5 dashes Bittermens Xocolatl Mole Bitters

Orange peel, for garnish

FORD

Inspiration: George J. Kappeler, *Modern American Drinks*, 1895

Like the Angelus (page 240), this is another 1890s gin and dry vermouth cocktail where the proportions are fifty-fifty. Fifty-fifty is a hell of a strong combination, and Jack has shown some mercy by sneaking in some sweeter, though of course still bone-dry, maraschino liqueur.

This is what a real cocktail is about: booze and bitters. Learn it, love it, live it.

DIRECTIONS

+ Add all the ingredients, except the garnish, to a mixing glass. Fill with ice and stir until chilled. Strain the mixture into a cocktail glass. Twist the orange peel over the glass to express the oils, then discard the peel.

INGREDIENTS

1½ ounces Tanqueray London Dry Gin

1½ ounces dry vermouth

½ ounce maraschino liqueur

3 dashes orange bitters

5 dashes Pernod Absinthe

Orange peel, for garnish

BIJOU

Inspiration: Harry Johnson, *Bartenders' Manual*, 1900

This gem lives up to its name. It is one of few from the archives that our Mr. McGarry has not changed very much, adjusting proportions rather than purpose. It is a big hit of gin and sweet vermouth, another fifty-fifty as was dominant in the period, although the original actually calls for one-third of each, plus a third of Chartreuse. Let's give those swell French monks a break and dial it back a bit. With the proportions now stabilized, feel free to have two.

DIRECTIONS

+ Add all the ingredients, except the garnish, to a mixing glass. Fill with ice and stir until chilled. Strain the mixture into a cocktail glass. Twist the orange peel over the glass to express the oils, then discard the peel.

INGREDIENTS

1½ ounces Tanqueray London Dry Gin

1½ ounces sweet vermouth

½ ounce Green Chartreuse

2 dashes orange bitters

2 dashes Dead Rabbit Orinoco Bitters or Angostura Aromatic Bitters

2 dashes Pernod Absinthe

Orange peel, for garnish

BLACKTHORN ROYAL

Inspiration: Hugo Ensslin, *Recipes for Mixed Drinks*, 1916

Unlike many of the early bartenders we've relied on, Hugo Ensslin was not particularly famous in his day. His book was self-published and never a success—so rare in later years, as David Wondrich notes in his introduction to its reprinting, "that nobody was actually looking for it."

But the book turns out to be a fine prize for both historians and imbibers, as Ensslin recounts within it many recipes which were thought to be created in later years, and often therefore attributed to their later chroniclers. By telling us what people were drinking in New York in 1916, Ensslin managed to scoop later, more popular books such as the *Savoy Cocktail Book* with at least (by Professor Wondrich's count) 146 recipes previously thought to have originated a decade later.

It's a no-nonsense booklet, firing off half a dozen recipes per page without stopping to chat about any of them. The Blackthorn, true to this utilitarian approach, is a fifty-fifty combo of sloe gin and sweet vermouth.

For our purposes, we will lend it regality through application of Champagne, and round out the stereotypically sweet sloe with headier notes from Jameson Black Barrel Whiskey and Bitter Truth Violet Liqueur. When selecting a sloe gin, however, you must go with the best on the market today, Plymouth. The same can be said for the sensitively nuanced Carpano Antica, vermouth so good one might swig it from the bottle.

⊰DIRECTIONS⊱

• Add all the ingredients, except the Champagne and garnish, to a mixing glass. Fill with ice and stir until chilled. Strain the mixture into an ice-filled punch glass. Add the Champagne. Twist the orange peel over the glass to express the oils, then discard the peel.

⊰INGREDIENTS⊱

1 ounce Plymouth Sloe Gin

¾ ounce Jameson Black Barrel Irish Whiskey

¾ ounce Carpano Antica Formula Sweet Vermouth

¼ ounce The Bitter Truth Violet Liqueur

2 dashes Bittermens Burlesque Bitters

1 ounce Piper-Heidsieck Cuvée Brut

Orange peel, for garnish

WEEPER'S JOY

Inspiration: William Schmidt, The Flowing Bowl, 1892

Points from the start for one of the most evocative monikers of any mixed drink. The Weeper's Joy is an incredibly dry, herbal beverage balanced with the marvelous Orchard Street Celery Shrub—part refreshing vinegar shrub, part ode to Dr. Brown's Cel-Ray soda.

You will laugh, you will cry, and you will have another.

DIRECTIONS

+ Add all the ingredients, except the garnish, to a mixing glass. Fill with ice and stir until chilled. Strain the mixture into a cocktail glass. Twist the orange peel over the glass to express the oils, then discard the peel.

INGREDIENTS

2 ounces dry vermouth

¾ ounce Kümmel

¼ ounce Bénédictine

¼ ounce Pernod Absinthe

3 dashes orange bitters

3 dashes Bittermens Orchard Street Celery Shrub

Orange peel, for garnish

DESHLER

Inspiration: Hugo Ensslin, *Recipes for Mixed Drinks*, 1916

Dave Deshler, a lightweight boxer active at the time of *Recipes for Mixed Drinks*, merited in its pages an interesting one-two punch of rye and Dubonnet. In this rematch, Jack has expanded the fortified wine into the botanic Contratto Rosso, the citric China China Amer, and the spicy Royal Combier. And he's added more rye, so let's call this Deshler a middleweight.

DIRECTIONS

+ Add all the ingredients, except the garnish, to a mixing glass. Fill with ice and stir until chilled. Strain the mixture into a cocktail glass. Twist the orange peel over the glass to express the oils, then discard the peel.

INGREDIENTS

1½ ounces Bulleit Rye

½ ounce Contratto Vermouth Rosso

½ ounce Bigallet China China Amer

¼ ounce Royal Combier

4 dashes Peychaud's Bitters

4 dashes Pernod Absinthe

Orange peel, for garnish

Memorialized by poets and painters, banned by governments, credited with hallucinogenic powers, and feared by the populace—just what is going on with absinthe?

Absinthe is a botanical spirit flavored with anise, fennel, and wormwood—the *Artemisia absinthium* from which it derives its name. Although it's often called a liqueur, strictly speaking those contain sugar. Absinthe does not, which may have added to its reputation as strong stuff. But the Mediterranean is full of anise-flavored spirits, as the plant is native to that region, including Greek ouzo, Italian sambuca, Turkish raki, and various Middle Eastern araks. What did absinthe do to become the scary one?

Mostly, what it did was grow and grow. According to legend, modern absinthe was first distilled around 1792 in Couvet, Switzerland, by a French doctor of the unlikely name of Pierre Ordinaire. Or perhaps he had merely received the recipe from others in town who had already been making it. But within a few years the formula was being produced not just in Couvet, but in France, by Pernod Fils, and its empire grew. By the 1860s, French cafés were full of absinthe drinkers, so much that the hour after work was known as *l'heure verte*, or the green hour, from the green-tinged spirit tipplers threw back by the millions of liters.

All that drinking, of course, and of a novelty beverage rather than culturally ingrained wine and brandy, drew the ire of the temperance movements. The Congo Free State was first to ban absinthe, in 1898, followed by Belgium and Brazil in 1906, the Netherlands in 1909, Switzerland in 1910, the United States in 1912, France in 1914, Germany in 1923, and Italy in 1926. Countries where it was never banned, such as the United Kingdom, were places it was never much favored to begin with.

Thus, absinthe had been singled out over any other alcoholic product for nationwide bans. As the Seattle-based Wormwood Society notes on their educational website, there wasn't much point in it. "Contrary to popular misconception, absinthe is not hallucinogenic, psychedelic, or narcotic. If you're looking for this kind of experience you'll be very disappointed in genuine absinthe. The only drug in absinthe is alcohol. . . . The legendary mind-altering effects of absinthe have been misleadingly attributed to thujone, a compound found in wormwood, but are more likely to have been caused by extreme alcoholism as well as the substandard preparations passed off as absinthe."

In the opening of the twenty-first century, absinthe began to return legally to Europe and, in 2007, to the United States. There are now many excellent brands available, so let's sample them in the historic styles of their heyday.

Please note that although absinthe drips, spoons, and other specialized equipment are often used to prepare the drink, we're demystifying our recipes by keeping them free of such absinthiana, lovely though it is. Your regular mixing glasses and shakers

ABSINTHE, SWISS STYLE

Inspiration: William T. Boothby, *Cocktail Boothby's American Bar-Tender*, 1891

The Swiss pioneered the stuff after all, so let's start here. "Cocktail Bill" Boothby humbly refers to adding almandine orgeat to absinthe as "a nice way" and we agree. Start with a Swiss brand of absinthe, and you're almost done just as you begin.

This is a straightforward recipe to bring out the flavors inherent in the absinthe, softened a bit with orgeat and lengthened with soda water.

DIRECTIONS

+ Add all the ingredients, except the soda water and garnish, to a mixing glass. Fill with ice and stir until chilled. Strain into a wine glass and add the chilled soda water. Twist the lemon peel over the glass to express the oils, then discard the peel.

INGREDIENTS

½ ounce Orgeat Syrup (see page 141)

2 ounces Duplais Verte Absinthe

2 ounces chilled soda water

Lemon peel, for garnish

ABSINTHE, ITALIAN STYLE

Inspiration: O. H. Byron, *The Modern Bartenders' Guide*, 1884

Byron's manual lists different national takes on absinthe preparation, including French and American. But the Italians take a different approach, including one (or more) of their own country's famed cordials in the mix.

For this drink, we'll combine French absinthe with Italian anise liquor from Varnelli, which unlike sambuca is very dry, and to round it off, perhaps a tiny addition of the famous Italian Fernet Branca Menta, a bold eucalyptus-based liqueur. Due to those components, the Italian style focuses on herbal flavors. This is a fine beverage to cover up any other beverage on your breath.

⊹⊞DIRECTIONS⊞⊹

✦ Add all the ingredients except the garnish to a mixing glass. Fill with ice and stir until chilled. Strain into a cocktail glass. Twist the lemon peel over the glass to express the oils, then discard the peel.

⊹⊞INGREDIENTS⊞⊹

1 teaspoon Sugar Syrup (see page 67)

¼ ounce Fernet Branca Menta

½ ounce Varnelli l'Anice Secco Speciale

1½ ounces Pernod Absinthe

1½ ounces chilled water

Lemon peel, for garnish

ABSINTHE, AMERICAN STYLE

Inspiration: George Winter, *How to Mix Drinks*, 1884

Since absinthe's return to legality in the United States, several native producers of quality have emerged. To celebrate this milestone as we continue our tour of nations, here's an all-American formulation of Californian St. George absinthe, water from your local tap (if American), and sugar syrup. (Although if you want to go extra American, substitute Froot Loops for the latter.)

The preparation style where water is directly mixed with absinthe, rather than dripped in slowly, is the American method, as opposed to the French. In our opinion, it turns out more balanced, so that is how each of these recipes has been presented, regardless of their national ingredients. (Also, it doesn't require any special absinthe plumbing in your bar area.)

This preparation is one of the simplest and easiest, designed to truly showcase the spirit itself.

❖ DIRECTIONS ❖

◆ Add all the ingredients to a mixing glass. Fill with ice and stir until chilled. Strain into a cocktail glass.

❖ INGREDIENTS ❖

½ ounce Sugar Syrup (see page 67)

2 ounces chilled water

2 ounces St. George Absinthe

ABSINTHE, FRENCH STYLE

Inspiration: Jerry Thomas, *The Bar-Tenders' Guide*, 1862

Jerry Thomas kept things simple; he felt absinthe and chilled water were enough. Jerry Thomas was not French.

While absinthe is enjoyed in many ways in every region where it's known, we couldn't decide on just one typical French style, because the French developed so many. So, instead, here's a do-it-yourself flatpack of absinthe. Start with Professor Thomas' half-and-half preparation, then add the sweetener of your choice, presented in the list below.

"Tomate" refers to the tomato-like color, not the flavor. Similarly, "Perroquet," or parrot, is for its vibrant green rather than any avian ingredients. "Mauresque," or Moorish, style is popular in the south of France, supposedly originated by soldiers who were sent off to fight in North Africa. "Rourou" appears to be baby talk for "rouge," red, for those too cool to order their absinthe with whole words. However, in times of emergency, the drink that can be called for with the fewest syllables can save a life, so we applaud this gloriously Gallic technique.

❖ DIRECTIONS ❖

+ Add all the ingredients to a mixing glass. Fill with ice and stir until chilled. Strain into a cocktail glass.

❖ INGREDIENTS ❖

2 ounces Pernod Absinthe

2 ounces chilled water

½ ounce desired sweetener

Lemon peel, for garnish

Sweetener Options (choose one)

> Regular: Sugar Syrup (see page 67)
>
> Tomate: Raspberry Cordial (see page 66)
>
> Perroquet: Marie Brizard Crème de Menthe
>
> Mauresque: Orgeat Syrup (see page 141)
>
> Rourou: Strawberry Cordial (see page 89)

ABSINTHE COCKTAIL

Inspiration: Harry Johnson, *Bartenders' Manual*, 1882

An elegant expression of the absinthe concept in cocktail form, this version of the Absinthe Cocktail (like the Absinthe, Italian Style, see page 262) again calls on Italian dry anise liquor and a second Italian liqueur, this time the equally dry cherry stone maraschino liqueur.

Absinthe is pervasive in New Orleans, so let's pull in homegrown Peychaud's bitters to add French Quarter style and offer contrast to the Orinoco and maraschino.

This drink is for the committed absinthe aficionado only. Serving it cocktail style means the water content is reduced and the strong absinthe flavors are at the fore. But that's the way it should be with this chic, classic concoction.

DIRECTIONS

+ Add all the ingredients, except the garnish, to a mixing glass. Fill with ice and stir until chilled. Strain into a cocktail glass. Twist the lemon peel over the glass to express the oils, then discard the peel.

INGREDIENTS

2 dashes Dead Rabbit Orinoco Bitters or Angostura Aromatic Bitters

2 dashes Peychaud's Bitters

¾ ounce chilled water

¼ ounce Luxardo Maraschino

½ ounce Varnelli l'Anice Secco Speciale

1½ ounces Vieux Pontarlier Absinthe

Lemon peel, for garnish

SUISSESSE

Inspiration: C. F. Lawlor, *The Mixicologist*, 1899

The culmination of absinthe in the mixed drink format is the Suissesse, a simple and delicious beverage that many (especially in New Orleans) select for their daily eye-opener. Typically made with cream and egg as a kind of absinthe milkshake, Jack's version is on another level. A drink so good that it transcends bartending and mixology, we had to consider it an example of that even rarer practice, Mixicology.

Christopher F. Lawlor, chief bartender of the Grand Hotel and Burnet House, Cincinnati, may be the only bartender to ever refer to himself as a Mixicologist, but we admire him for it. We also like that he calls his version of this drink the "Swiss S.," so that its pronunciation will be no obstacle for his American audience.

When you are in the Crescent City, stop by the Old Absinthe House for a creamy Suissesse. In the meantime, try Jack's reimagined version which substitutes cream for seeds: caraway and chocolate. It's Mixicologically magical.

⊰DIRECTIONS⊱

✦ Add all the ingredients, except the garnishes, to a shaker. Fill with ice and shake. Strain into a cocktail glass and garnish with freshly grated nutmeg. Twist the lemon peel over the glass to express the oils, then discard the peel.

⊰INGREDIENTS⊱

2 ounces chilled water

½ large egg white

2 dashes Peychaud's Bitters

½ ounce Linie Aquavit

½ ounce Marie Brizard Crème de Cacao

1½ ounces La Clandestine Absinthe

Fresh nutmeg, grated, for garnish

Lemon peel, for garnish

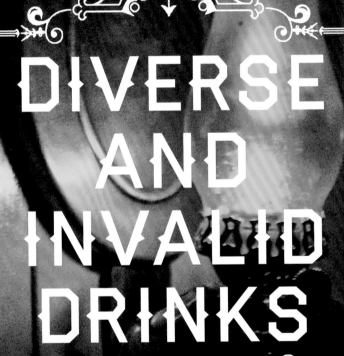

DIVERSE
AND
INVALID
DRINKS

O

ur miscellaneous category draws its inspiration from the nineteenth-century category of "invalid drinks"—preparations for the ill, rather than beverages that are baseless or unsound. Many of these were based on beer, as that was almost food anyway. So while there may be an early twenty-first century buzz over *micheladas* and other beer mixed drinks, know that these things come in cycles.

We have even sneaked in a nonalcoholic drink for all of the history and none of the regret. Just one, of course. You don't want to overdo it.

PORTER SANGAREE

Inspiration: Jerry Thomas, *The Bar-Tenders' Guide*, 1862

In the early nineteenth century, sangarees were made from wine or beer, plus sugar, water, and nutmeg, and were considered a light beverage suitable for serving to children, the ill, and even those in recovery from alcoholism. Please follow your own moral compass regarding such service, but we can certainly recommend it to healthy, nondipsomaniac persons who have reached their majority.

Originally featuring Spanish fortified wines such as Madeira and sherry, the drink's name comes from *sangre*, for its blood color. (But not from sangría, which was invented later.) Perhaps the association with blood gave it a health context, or perhaps it was the inclusion of sugar, as in the julep (see our chapter on that drink and its medicinal history), but in America, ale and porter became commonly substituted for quotidian imbibing.

The molasses of the porter is lightened with use of Lemon Sherbet, and rounded with our herbal tincture and bitters. A "good and very wholesome Beverage," as stated by the *Boston Intelligencer* in 1819. Try it on a hot summer's day.

DIRECTIONS

• Add all the ingredients, except the garnishes, to a mixing glass. Fill with ice and stir until chilled. Strain into a punch glass with one chunk of ice. Garnish with freshly grated nutmeg. Twist the lemon peel over the glass to express the oils, then discard the peel.

INGREDIENTS

3 dashes Mace Tincture (see page 77)

¾ ounce Lemon Sherbet (see page 71)

3 dashes Dead Rabbit Orinoco Bitters or Angostura Aromatic Bitters

6 ounces Founders Porter

Fresh nutmeg, grated, for garnish

Lemon peel, for garnish

ELDERBERRY BEER À LA BYRON

Inspiration: O. H. Byron, *The Modern Bartenders' Guide*, 1884

With this recipe, we have tamed all dimensions of time and space. In Byron's original, he recommends starting with twenty gallons of wort, the liquid extracted from mashing grain, which has not yet fermented and so is not yet beer. Then he suggests boiling half a bushel of elderberries and introducing that to the mixture. Securing all into a barrel, in a year's time you will have your Elderberry Beer. Quoth Byron, "You will be surprised at the result." Perhaps because you'll have forgotten what that barrel was for by then.

If you are lacking a warehouse, easy wort access, or a year to find out if you like this drink, Jack offers the following reimagining, which brings elderberry (actually, the flower of the same plant) together with ale without barrels and within seconds.

DIRECTIONS

+ Fill one shaker with ice. Fill a second shaker with all the ingredients except the garnishes. Roll between the two shakers seven times, or until chilled (for a note on rolling, see page 193).

+ Strain into a wine glass. Garnish with freshly grated nutmeg. Twist the orange

INGREDIENTS

3 dashes Elderberry Tincture (see recipe at right)

3 dashes Dead Rabbit Orinoco Bitters or Angostura Aromatic Bitters

¼ ounce Varnelli Anis

1¼ ounces Chase Elderflower Liqueur

6 ounces cask ale

Fresh nutmeg, grated, for garnish

Orange peel, for garnish

ELDERBERRY TINCTURE

✦ Combine the elderberries and Everclear in a jar. Allow to macerate for 3 days, then strain through a chinois into a fresh container. Add the water. Due to the alcohol content, this tincture should last indefinitely at room temperature.

1 ounce crushed, dried elderberries

4½ ounces Everclear

4½ ounces water

YIELDS *About 10 ounces*

SHANDYGAFF

Inspiration: Harry Johnson, *Bartenders' Manual*, 1882

As our cousins on the mean streets of Britain know, a shandy is a beer mixed with lemon soda or ginger ale. And here is its progenitor from the nineteenth century. According to British drink encyclopedia *Difford's Guide*, "[t]he name comes from the London slang for a pint of beer, 'shant of gatter' (shanty being a public house, gatter meaning water). The ginger ale serves as a flavoursome way to water down the strength of the beer, thus the literal translation, 'pub water.'"

Our version of pub water eschews ginger ale for lime soda and ginger syrup, making it both citrus and ginger, all the types of shandy at once. The syrup, of course, pushes the ginger forward, but the soda and orange curaçao turn up the brightness to support it. The malty Fuller's brings a bitter edge.

You may try to teach this recipe to the landlord at your local pub, but under no circumstances include the term "pub water."

⊰ DIRECTIONS ⊱

✦ Fill one shaker with ice. Fill a second shaker with all the ingredients except the garnishes. Roll between the two shakers seven times, or until chilled (for a note on rolling, see page 193).

✦ Strain into a tall glass. Garnish with freshly grated nutmeg. Twist the lime peel over the glass to express the oils, then discard the peel.

⊰ INGREDIENTS ⊱

1 ounce Ginger Syrup (see page 118)

½ ounce fresh lime juice

3 ounces wild lime soda

3 ounces Fuller's ESB

¾ ounce Pierre Ferrand Dry Orange Curaçao

3 dashes Dead Rabbit Orinoco Bitters or Angostura Aromatic Bitters

Fresh nutmeg, grated, for garnish

Lime peel, for garnish

VELVET GAFF

Inspiration: William T. Boothby, *The World's Drinks and How to Mix Them*, 1908

The original recipe calls for Dublin stout and Champagne (sometimes also called a Black Velvet), but let's keep this on the beer tip by substituting sparkling cider. And, yes, okay, some booze for good measure.

The rich, dark porter plus the effervescent, crisp cider is what makes this "velvet." Pear liqueur then expands on the orchard flavors, and where there are apples and pears we're happy to introduce spices from mace, nutmeg, and our own Orinoco bitters. Why is there gin added to this? Ask your cheerful Aunt Clarice.

❦ DIRECTIONS ❦

✦ Add all the ingredients, except the garnishes, to a mixing glass. Fill with ice and stir until chilled. Strain into an ice-filled tall glass. Garnish with freshly grated nutmeg. Twist the lemon peel over the glass to express the oils, then discard the peel.

❦ INGREDIENTS ❦

3 dashes Mace Tincture (see page 77)

4 ounces Christian Drouin Cidre Bouche

3 ounces Founders Porter

¾ ounce Plymouth Gin

¾ ounce Merlet Crème de Poire

3 dashes Dead Rabbit Orinoco Bitters or Angostura Aromatic Bitters

Fresh nutmeg, grated, for garnish

Lemon peel, for garnish

ITALIAN LEMONADE

Inspiration: Jerry Thomas, *The Bar-Tenders' Guide*, 1862

Thomas combines lemonade and sherry to make Italian Lemonade. But why is it Italian? Because of the deep history of the "limonadiers" of that nation. As the inimitable David Wondrich elucidates in *Punch*: "The Italians in general and Neapolitans and Sicilians in particular had spent generations perfecting the art of making iced sherbets chilled with the snow that lingered year-round in sections of the Italian peninsula's mountainous spine—delicate, refreshing things that were between water and snow in texture and nectar and ambrosia in flavor."

Jack's modern take is a cavalcade of the produce of tree, bush, and vine. Lemon sherbet replaces both sugar and lemon juice, and the liquidity comes from orange juice, orange flower water, and orange soda. Body arrives with raspberry eau de vie and the delicately dry, almost salty, Manzanilla.

See if you can tell if it's more like nectar or ambrosia.

DIRECTIONS

✦ Add all the ingredients, except the orange soda and garnishes, to a shaker. Fill with ice and shake. Strain into an ice-filled tall glass. Add the orange soda. Twist the orange peel over the glass to express the oils, then discard the peel. Do the same with the lemon peel.

INGREDIENTS

1 ounce Lemon Sherbet (see page 71)

1½ ounces Barbadillo Manzanilla Sherry

1½ ounces F. Meyer Framboise Eau de Vie

1 ounce orange juice

1 dash orange flower water

1½ ounces blood orange soda

Orange peel, for garnish

Lemon peel, for garnish

BRUNSWICK COOLER
NONALCOHOLIC

Inspiration: O. H. Byron, *The Modern Bartenders' Guide*, 1884

This is another example of changing ginger ale into something just a bit more. Using plain soda water, and a couple of the syrups you've already made for other drinks in this book (plus, okay, one tincture that you have to make especially for it), you have the perfect nonalcoholic refresher for down times or for those who have yet to step up to our way of drinking. And, of course, invalids.

We predict the Brunswick Cooler will be showing up at finer baby showers come springtime.

⁖DIRECTIONS⁖

* Add all the ingredients, except the soda water and garnish, to a shaker. Fill with ice and shake. Add the soda water. Strain into an ice-filled tall glass and garnish with freshly grated nutmeg.

⁖INGREDIENTS⁖

7 dashes Coriander Tincture (see recipe below)

1 ounce Ginger Syrup (see page 118)

¾ ounce Lemon Sherbet (see page 71)

1¼ ounces fresh lemon juice

4 ounces soda water

Fresh nutmeg, grated, for garnish

CORIANDER TINCTURE

* Combine the coriander and Everclear in a jar. Allow to macerate for 3 days, then strain through a chinois into a fresh container. Add the water. Due to the alcohol content, this tincture should last indefinitely at room temperature.

1 ounce ground coriander

4½ ounces Everclear

4½ ounces water

YIELDS *About 14 ounces*

IRISH COFFEE

Inspiration: The Buena Vista Café, San Francisco, California, 1952

There are those who wish us to believe the unlikely fact that Irish Coffee was invented at Shannon Airport in the 1940s. Obviously, for any of us who have been to any airport, we know that nothing creative has ever occurred in such a place.

A competing tale has it that Jonathan Swift invented the Irish Coffee in 1705 through the simple genius of adding whiskey to his coffee and cream. Earlier the same day he had invented the Irish toasted cheese, Irish biscuit, Irish hat stand, and Irish stack of envelopes by inadvertently pouring whiskey onto those household items as well.

Regardless of its original production, the drink did not come into its own until its appearance in San Francisco at the Buena Vista Café, where it became a permanent favorite of locals and tourists alike. We always knew we wanted an Irish Coffee on the menu at the Dead Rabbit, as it is perhaps the best-known Irish-American classic, and this recipe was designed under the guidance of Dale "King Cocktail" DeGroff. It's a deceptively simple approach. One secret: Buy ridiculously expensive heavy cream from your favorite local dairy.

Another tip: When preparing this classic, be careful not to slip on the Irish floor.

DIRECTIONS

+ Add all the ingredients, except the garnish, to an Irish coffee glass. Float an inch of whipped cream on top. Garnish with freshly grated nutmeg.

INGREDIENTS

½ ounce Demerara Sugar Syrup (see page 281)

1½ ounces Powers Gold Label Irish Whiskey

4 ounces hot filtered coffee

1 ounce whipped heavy cream, for garnish

Fresh nutmeg, grated, for garnish

DEMERARA SUGAR SYRUP

✦ Combine the sugar and water in a medium saucepan over medium heat, but do not boil. Slowly stir to dissolve the sugar. When the syrup has thickened, remove from the heat. Use a funnel to pour into bottles. The syrup will keep for 2 to 3 weeks in the refrigerator.

2 cups granulated Demerara sugar

2 cups water

YIELDS *About 16 ounces*

INDEX

International barman **Sean Muldoon** is the cofounder and managing partner of the Dead Rabbit Grocery and Grog in New York City, and formerly the bar manager of the Merchant Hotel in Belfast. The Merchant was declared "World's Best Cocktail Bar" in 2010 at Tales of the Cocktail, and the Dead Rabbit won three awards at Tales of the Cocktail 2013, including "World's Best New Cocktail Bar." In 2014, the Dead Rabbit won two further awards at the event, including "Best American Cocktail Bar." The Dead Rabbit is the expression of Sean's lifelong dream to combine sophisticated cocktail service with the rich tradition of the Anglo-Hibernian pub.

In his roles at both the Dead Rabbit, of which he is a cofounder and managing partner, and the Merchant Hotel, **Jack McGarry** became internationally known for his extensive historically based beverage programs. Immediately prior to joining the Dead Rabbit, Jack tended bar at Milk & Honey London, one of the world's most highly awarded bar operations. In July 2013, Jack was honored with the prestigious Tales of the Cocktail International Bartender of the Year award. He is its youngest ever recipient, and only the second in America.

Ben Schaffer has been "the voice" of the Dead Rabbit since even before its launch, writing all its promotional material. In November 2012, Ben cofounded consulting firm The Best Bar in the World with Sean Muldoon and Jack McGarry, to offer their hospitality expertise worldwide. He is currently adapting Alasdair Gray's novel *1982 Janine* for the stage.